Sheffield — Langsett

64 Langsett Road 1905.
Herbert Smith is standing in the doorway with his 6 year old son, Allan.
He moved into this shop in 1905 and it was kept until 1937.

Smith's Cycle Shops
1890-1967

and the original

![Sheffield - Langsett]

bicycle

Head transfer 1939-1962.

Stuart Smith

To Carole

— LANGSETT "SHEFFIELD" LIGHTWEIGHT. —

Can be built with Off Set or Gradual Rake Front Forks to order.

From R.A. & E.S. Smith's 1938 catalogue.

ISBN: 978-0-901100-95-5

Designed and printed by
Northend Creative Print Solutions
Clyde Road, Sheffield S8 0TZ
keith@northend.co.uk
emma@northend.co.uk
www.northend.co.uk

CONTENTS

LANGSETT CYCLING SHOES.

LANGSETT CYCLING SHOES ARE MADE FROM THE BEST LEATHER OBTAINABLE BY MOBBS OF KETTERING, MAKERS OF THE FAMOUS "EMBEKAY" SPORTS SHOES.

Each shoe fitted with protecting leather
side patch.

Sizes stocked :

5, 6, 6½, 7, 7½, 8, 8½, 9, 9½, and 10.

All weather.
Fitted with broad elastic band under
flap, ensuring perfect fit.
Price **12/6** per pair.
Black only.

Club Shoe.
A very neat, light shoe, suitable for
general use. Fitted with long flap tongue.
Price **12/6** per pair.
Black only.

All weather.
Fitted with U-skide inlaid heel piece.
Elastic band under flap, a very
comfortable shoe.
Price **13/6** per pair.
Black only.

Langsett T.F. Bailey Shoe.
Fitted with long flap tongue. Rich brown,
trimmed with black. Toe piece specially
designed and strengthened to relieve pressure if toe clips are used. Very supple and
comfortable to wear. Plyable instep.
Designed by a cyclist for a cyclist.

Price **12/6** per pair.

Popular Shoe.
Made from good black leather. Strong
heel and sole.
A popular shoe at a popular price.
Price **8/6** per price.

SHOES SENT CARRIAGE PAID ANYWHERE IN GREAT BRITAIN.

LANGSETT CYCLING CLOTHING.

TWO-PIECE PLUS-FOUR CYCLING SUITS.

Jackets Lined, cut to latest style, 3 Pockets. Plus-Fours, Full Cut, Double
seated, Buckle under knee. All Suits made to Special Measure.

The Clubman Suit to measure 2 piece 32/6.
„ Tourist „   „   „   2 „ 40/-.
„ Yorkshire „   „   „   2 „ 52/-.

PLUS-FOURS WITH DOUBLE SEAT.

Full cut, Made of Rich Brown, Heather and Grey Mottled Tweeds.

Waist Sizes : 30, 32, 34 and 36. Prices 14/6, 16/6, 19/6 per pair.

LADIES RATIONALS PLUS-FOUR STYLE.

The latest cut to special measure, Jackets lined, 3 pockets, Plus-Fours full
cut double seated, Buckle under knee.

The Clubgirl Suit, to measure. 2 piece 32/6.
„ Tourist „   „   „   2 „ 40/-.
„ Yorkshire „   „   „   2 „ 52/ .

PLUS-FOURS WITH DOUBLE SEAT.

Full cut, made of Rich Brown, Heather and Grey Mottled Tweeds. to
Special Measure.

Prices 14/6, 16/6 and 19/6 per pair.

From the 1933 catalogue.

Introduction

Cycling was an important part of my father's family from the time my grandfather, Herbert Smith, bought his first 'penny-farthing' in 1883. He produced the original 'Langsett Lightweight', and his shop and business were the foundation for the successful firm built up by my father, Edward, and his brother, Allan. Although I am not a 'true cyclist', I have always had a keen interest in the design and engineering of bicycles.

In 1947 my grandfather wrote about his early cycling days and the start of the business in 1890, and I feel it appropriate to include this story in full as written in his own words. In my younger days I mastered the riding of the family's penny-farthing which was exhilarating and great fun; it was also very good to ride on smooth level roads and I have much affection for these machines. Riding on cobbled streets or over pot-holes was not so good and I can relate with sympathy to my grandfather's early adventures, especially the learning to ride experiences!

My most enjoyable and fastest rides have been on the marvellous Moulton bicycle, which I have had the good fortune to do with Dr. Alex Moulton on many occasions. This advanced engineering bicycle is the best touring bicycle ever produced and none other can compare with its comfort and efficiency. Bicycles are remarkable and extraordinary devices and their development is as fascinating to me now as it would have been in my grandfather's day.

This first book outlines the story of my family's cycle business up to the time the Infirmary Road shop was sold in 1967. I have also included details of the framesets built in our workshop in the 1950s, and illustrations of the transfers which were applied.

R. A. & E. S. SMITH.

SHEFFIELD

TELEPHONE 43401

MAKERS OF THE **LANGSETT** LIGHTWEIGHT **CYCLE**

MAKERS OF THE **LANGSETT** LIGHTWEIGHT **TANDEM**

LANGSETTS LAST LONGEST

OFFICIAL REPAIRER TO THE

LANGSETT CYCLE

OFFICIAL REPAIRER TO THE

OFFICE AND SHOWROOM

64, LANGSETT ROAD,

WORKS

BERTHA STREET,

SOME OF THE SOLDIERS SUPPLIED WITH "LANGSETT" CYCLES 29 YEARS AGO

80,000 Miles on a "Langsett."

February 2nd, 1932.

Dear Sirs,

I feel that you are entitled to some praise for the "Langsett Lightweight" you built up to my Specification during February 1923.

During **80,000** miles of **strenuous cycling** I have **never once** been let down by this wonderful little machine.

I can highly recommend your machines for any phase of cycling and will do so whenever I have chance.

Yours truly,

J.T.L.

1872

1869

BOWNS & CO PRINTERS, GRANVILLE ST SHEFFIELD.

The Langsett bicycle models featured in the 1932 catalogue were the 'Chater-Lea Sports', 'Vulcan', 'Spartan', 'Chromium Sports', 'Light Tourer' and Tandems.

The story of the Langsett bicycle

1890-1925 – Herbert Smith, the early days

The Langsett bicycle was originated in 1895 by my grandfather, Herbert Smith. It was the first B.S.A. Lightweight in Sheffield. He describes it as 'short wheelbase, 26 inch wheels and 21 lbs weight'. It enabled him to do well in the Sheffield Central Cycling Club competition events and led to orders for similar machines and trade for his well known cycle shop. The shop was on Langsett Road in Sheffield and he called the bicycle the 'Langsett', in later years it became known as the 'Sheffield-Langsett'.

Herbert was born in Watery Lane in Sheffield in 1866, the son of a pocket knife blade grinder. Although he had little formal education he had a natural aptitude for practical metalworking and worked in the Sheffield silversmith and knife blade trades from an early age. His interest in art and design is evident from his painting and photography. Cycling became the centre of his life from the day he bought his 'ordinary' or 'penny-farthing' bicycle when he was seventeen years old in 1883. Although this one was too big for him he managed to ride it, and this was soon replaced by one of a suitable size which he rode as often as he could with friends or by himself. He was a great enthusiast of the 'big wheel' bicycle and this type of machine took him on many memorable rides into Derbyshire and to Newark, Doncaster and Lincoln; in 1886 he rode to Boston and back in the day. At first he disparaged the new 'safety' bicycles, but in 1892 after nine years of riding ordinaries he finally acquired one. An active member of the Sheffield Central Cycling Club from its beginning in 1892, he was treasurer for many years. His competition successes included second place and the Silver Medal in the Yorkshire Road Club time trial from York to Retford in 1897.

At that time local blacksmiths were often used by cyclists, but Herbert was able to use his experience and ability to carry out his own repairs and used these skills to open his first cycle shop in 1890 on Springvale Road, and a workshop on Penistone Road. Shortly afterwards the shop moved to number 73 on nearby Langsett Road, which gave the name to the bicycles. Sales of cycles in the shop were supplemented with various items of hardware, toys, and later the new gramophone and records. In 1903 a good order for twelve bicycles came from the nearby army barracks which helped his reputation and he sold more bicycles to soldiers during

Herbert Smith in a 1931 advertisement for Constrictor cycle parts.

The 'Chromium Sports' model in 1931.

the following years. In 1905 the shop moved across the road to number 64 Langsett Road where it would stay until 1937, with the workshop round the corner at Bertha Street. The new 'lightweight' frames used high quality thin walled steel tubing but at that time cycle parts – screw threads and sizes – were not uniform which made replacements and repairs difficult and so Herbert built his Langsett Lightweight models with the new 'B.S.A. Standard' fittings. He was also the agent for the Fleet Bicycle which he rode in competitive events for advertising purposes.

In later life he still enjoyed his cycling with long tours including Cornwall, Wales and Scotland, riding the Langsett bicycle which he had built for himself. He was cycling until only a few years before his death in 1954 aged 87.

The 1920s-1930s – R.A. & E.S. Smith

In 1926 Herbert's two sons, Rupert Allan Smith and my father, Edward Stuart Smith, continued the business as 'R.A. & E.S. Smith', manufacturers of the Sheffield Langsett bicycle in the same shop at 64 Langsett Road. R.A. and E.S. – 'Allan' and 'Edward' – were both talented and accomplished riders prominent in the Sheffield Central Cycling Club. Both brothers were gifted artists and designers, Allan was the Sheffield Central C.C. Race Secretary and organised many club runs and events. His experience as a draughtsman in a Sheffield drawing office enabled him to produce excellent drawings and route maps. He designed all the 'Langsett' transfers, catalogues and displays and his original fine artwork was used for all of these. Edward's practical skills and desire for perfection ensured the high quality of the bicycles from this period. Their creative thinking also ensured original displays in the shop window. In addition to cycles, the shop had a good trade in the sales and repair of gramophones, especially the Sheffield-made Gilbert. Between 1923 and 1926 Edward was successful in many time trials, winning medals in the N.C.U. Road Championships and Sheffield C.C.C. events. Eveline Smith *(later to become Eveline MacDougall)*, my aunt and sister to Allan and Edward, was the S.C.C.C. Social Secretary and featured in club outings and events. This must have been a 'golden age' of the family bicycle firm which embraced a considerable social and sporting calendar.

The 1930s catalogues show developments, innovations and a wide range of models. The move to the Infirmary Road shop half a mile down the main road towards the city centre meant that the address was no longer 'Langsett' Road, and at that time the Bertha Street workshop was moved, so that 182/184 Infirmary Road became the head office and workshop.

The Infirmary Road shop just after the War in 1945.

Record sleeve 1927.

The old shop at 64 Langsett Road was kept until 1937 when the business was able to occupy the whole block of shops at 182 to 192 Infirmary Road. In 1935 a second shop was opened at 53-55 West Street in the city centre. Several contracts to supply heavy duty bicycles to the Sheffield Police Force were obtained during this period.

The 1940s – Langsett Lightweight Cycles Ltd

In 1942 the firm became Langsett Lightweight Cycles Limited and the particular skills required for building lightweight cycle frames were put to good use during the Second World War. Rose Brothers at Gainsborough manufactured the gun turrets for R.A.F. bombers and they needed a supplier of accurately made sights for the guns. These were made in the Langsett workshop at Infirmary Road. The close relationship with Rose Brothers continued after the War when their Gainsborough factory returned to the manufacture of automatic wrapping machines for the tobacco and confectionery industries, and because of the demand for these, Edward and Allan were able to obtain orders as sub-contractors for some of this work and then building some of the machines and so provide continued employment for the workshop staff. This in turn led to the expansion of the business as precision engineers. My father's cousin, Cyril King ('Uncle Cyril' to me when I was young) turned his skilled hands from cycles to brazing and silver soldering special engineering parts. I remember as a child travelling with my father to Gainsborough on a number of occasions in the Austin Ten which Allan and Edward shared, urgent parts on the back seat. In 1947, this was exchanged for a lovely 1930s drop-head Daimler. With the hood down it was possible to carry quite large items. Eventually the firm acquired a small 30 cwt van, but the heavy finished machines were collected by Rose Brothers' green painted Ford Thames lorries. I enjoyed travelling in the back of the van when I was ten years old, sitting on the rear wheel arch and trying not to slide off going round corners.

The "Langsett" Road Racer.

———— "Popular" Model. ————

BUILT OF BRAMPTON FITTINGS.

STANDARD SPECIFICATION :

FRAME—Brampton throughout, Renolds butted or A. and P. tubes brazed up back.

TOP STAYS—Straight, round, tapered.

BOTTOM STRUTS—Straight, Round, Tapered.

FRONT FORKS—Solid fork ends, slotted for drop-out, D to round.

REAR FORK ENDS—Forward or standard pattern.

PEDALS—Phillips, Race or Road.

SADDLE—Mansfield, Racing.

HANDLEBAR—Continental.

WHEELS—Dunlop rims, double butted spokes, Brampton superb hubs.

TYRES—Constrictor Python.

BRAKE—Front or rear.

CHAIN—Brampton or Perry's.

TRANSMISSION—Special cotterless bottom bracket, gear to order.

FINISH—Best black, short or long wheel base.

CASH PRICE £6 10 0.

Gradual Payment arranged. 14/- deposit and 3/6 per week for 44 weeks.

FRAME £3 5 0

Brampton throughout with Williams Chain-wheel and Cranks.

Ride a Langsett, Light and Rigid.

The Road Racer from the 1925 Langsett catalogue.
Other models include the Road or Path Racer £10-10-0,
Ladies' Sports Models at £6-10-0, and Gents' Roadsters from £5-5-0.
Saxon, Swift, Cheylesmore, Rudge-Whitworth and Raleigh cycles are
also listed.

Langsett Chater-Lea Sports.

Excellence in workmanship and high-class components combine to make the Langsett Chater-Lea the finest Lightweight built to-day. Please make your own choice from the first-class fittings offered which are manufactured by the leading firms in the cycling industry.

CHOICE OF FITTINGS.

FRAME—Chater-Lea fittings throughout, built with light chrome-molybdenum tubing, large ball bearings $\frac{5}{16}$" diameter in Bottom Bracket, ensuring easy pedalling under every condition, bracket height $10\frac{1}{2}$", wheelbase 42" or to order, Chater-Lea Chainwheel 40, 42, 44, 46, 48 or 52 teeth, Cranks $6\frac{1}{2}$ $6\frac{3}{4}$ or 7" to order.   HEAD large ball bearing $\frac{3}{16}$" dia. ensuring easy steering and taking away undue strain, expander bolt fitting, (head clip to order), Front Fork chrome-molybdenum steel, round or "D" to round, made to order straight, semi-straight or raked, solid ends.   Seat Pillar straight 'L' pattern or curved to order, chain adjusters fitted to rear fork ends if ordered.

LUBRICATION—2 oilers in head, 1 in bracket, force feed.

FINISH—Best cellulose, Panhard red, dark, medium or light blue, bright red or cream, front fork chromium plated tips or all over, rear fork ends chromium plated 6" on chain and seat stays 5/- extra if ordered, brazed on fittings, pump pegs, reflector clip, mudguard eyes etc.

HUBS—Chater-Lea disc adjusting, solid spindle fitted with dust proof caps (double cog rear).

SPOKES—Black, best quality, double butted.

COGS—Number of teeth to order.

RIMS—Light gauge Endrick, or narrow section Constrictor Westwood.

BRAKE—Constrictor Viper or Perry Internal expanding hub brake front or rear.

CHAIN—Perry or Coventry roller.

SADDLE—Brooks B17 standard, narrow or sprinter, Terry C.T.C. or Dunlop.

HANDLEBAR—Any style, celluloid covered to order, fitted with light-weight adjustable clip, 1 2 or 3" extension.

HANDLE GRIPS—Constrictor or Shockstop sponge rubber.

PEDALS—Chater Lea road or race.

MUDGUARDS Bluemel's New Noweight, or narrow section lightweight with or without extension.

EQUIPMENT—Bluemel's prismatic reflector, Pumpeesi pump and oil gun.

Nett Cash Price £11 15 0. All plated parts Chromium plated.

Terms : £2 18 0 deposit and 57 weekly payments of 3/6 or 11 monthly payments of 18/-.
Frame—Nett Cash Price £5 19 6 Terms arranged.

Nett Cash Price £11 5 0. All plated parts Nickel plated.

Terms : £2 8 0 deposit and weekly or monthly payments as above
Frame—Nett Cash Price £5 10 0 Terms arranged.

The best of the 1932 Langsett bicycle models. Others included the 'Vulcan', 'Spartan', 'Chromium Sports' and the 'Light Tourer'.

15

Illustrating Double Gents. straight drive, central stay.

Langsett Tandems.

First introduced to the Cycling World 36 years ago.   This speaks for itself !

FRAME--Built with Chater-Lea or Brampton fittings, double gent.'s or lady back to order.   The standard Chater-Lea model is the central stay design, but any other Chater-Lea type will be built to order (no extra charge) The Brampton can be built with central stay or twin lateral stays to order. TUBING USED: Reynolds' butted "A" quality throughout.   THE DRIVE on the Chater-Lea is the cross-over, No. 14 fittings, (illustrated on the left) or straight according to order, the cross over type has a $1\frac{1}{2}$" chain line and is very easy to adjust by means of the peg illustrated, also a shorter wheelbase may be obtained if desired, both assemblies of chainwheels are standard and interchangeable, (see illustration on the right) showing the adapter used on the straight drive to make this possible, number of teeth on chainwheels to order, the Brampton Tandem is fitted with a straight drive, number of teeth on chainwheels 52, 48 or 46 drive and 42 on small wheels, $\frac{5}{16}$" ball bearings in bottom brackets.

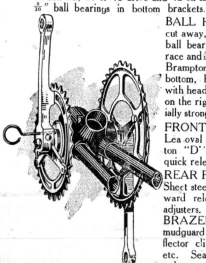

BALL HEAD— Lugs cut away, Chater-Lea $\frac{3}{16}$" ball bearings in the top race and $\frac{3}{16}$" in the bottom, Brampton $\frac{1}{4}$" top and bottom, both are fitted with head clip (illustrated on the right) and a specially strong $1\frac{1}{8}$" stem.

FRONT FORKS Chater-Lea oval to round, Brampton "D" to round, solid quick release ends.

REAR FORK ENDS— Sheet steel forward or backward release, fitted with chain adjusters.   All special parts BRAZED ON, pump clips, mudguard eyes, brake parts, reflector clip, chainrest, gear parts etc.   Seat Pillars according to order.

FRAMES.

Chater-Lea Nett Cash Price £11 17 6 Usual parts Nickel pla'ed.
    ,,   ,,   ,,   ,, £12 17 6 ,, ,, Chromium ,,
Brampton ,,   ,,   ,, £9 15 0 ,, ,, ,,   ,,
    Easy Payments : £3 0 0 deposit and 5/- weekly until paid.

1932 tandems.

Illustrating Cross-Over Drive Model fitted with Derailleur Gear and Hub Brakes.

Langsett Tandems.

WHEELS—Endrick or Westwood rims, 26 x 1¼" or 26 x 1⅜" Chater-Lea hubs, solid spindle, disc adjusting, Brampton with locked cones, double cog rear, fixed or free. Special care is taken with the building, black tandem spokes are used.

GEARS—To order,

TYRES—Dunlop or Palmer Tandem, or to order.

BRAKES—Resilion or Constrictor rim brakes or hub brakes accord'ng to choice, front and rear hub brakes are quick release. rear fitted with rod and lever which ensures quick action 2 brakes are fitted, (extra brakes will be charged for according to choice).

SADDLES—Brookes, Terry's C.T.C. or Dunlop.

CHAINS—Perry or Coventry.

PEDALS—Roadster, racing or rubber.

HANDLEBARS—Black celluloid covered fitted to lightweight adjustable clip. (type according to order, see accessory list, handlebar page).

MUDGUARDS—Bluemel's Noweight, Lightweight or Featherweight.

WHEELBASE—To order.

OILING—Tecalemit force feed.

EQUIPMENT—Bluemel's Prismatic reflector, Pumpeesi pump and Tecalemit oil gun.

FINISH—Best cellulose black or colour, (Panhard or bright red, light, medium or dark blue or cream) front forks chromium plated all over, no extra charged.

EXTRAS—Sturmey Archer or Perry 3 speed and hub brake 20/- extra, Cyclo or Pelissier Derailleur 3 speed 30/- 2 speed 27/6 extra, Sturmey Archer 3 speed 20/- extra.

CHATER-LEA.

Nett Cash Price £19 19 6. Usual parts Nickel plated.
Easy payments : £5 0 0 deposit and 5/- weekly until paid

Nett Cash Price £21 0 0. Usual parts Chromium plated.
Easy payments: £5 0 0 deposit and 5/- weekly until paid.

BRAMPTON.

Nett Cash Price £16 16 0. Usual parts Chromium pla.ed
Easy payments : £4 0 0 deposit and 5/- weekly until paid.
5% extra charged for easy payments.

We hold Sole Agency rights for Sheffield and district for
Stenton Glider Tandems £14 14 0.

Agents for GRUBB, SAXON, MERLIN, SELBACH, and SUN TANDEMS. Any make tandem supplied to order.

1932 tandems.

Can be built with Off Set or Gradual Rake Front Forks to order.

Nett Cash Price **£12 - 12 - 0** Built to Own Specification.

Easy Terms. 42/- Deposit and 62 Weekly Payments of 4/-.

CHOICE OF FITTINGS.

FRAME: Special Langsett Track Angles. Built with 531 Reynolds Butted Tubing, Track Rear Ends. Frame Size and Wheel Base to Order.

FORKS: 531 Butted Blade, Special Path Rake.

WHEELS: Constrictor Conloy Rims, Constrictor Light Steel or Solite Hubs, Wide Flange.

TUBULARS: Dunlop Path.

BARS: To Order.

PEDALS: Boa, B.S.A. or Webb.

TRANSMISSION: Williams 1″ Pitch Chainwheel and Cranks, Block Chain 1″ x $\frac{1}{8}$″ or $\frac{3}{16}$″.

SADDLE: Brooks Sprinter or to Choice.

EQUIPMENT: Tecalemit Oil Gun and Tools. Chater-Lea or B.S.A. Chainwheel and Cranks 12/6 extra charge.

Built with Special Langsett Lugs and Interiors.

SPECIAL TRACK FINISH

as Sheffield Model.

Frame and Fork Chromium Plated all over 10/- Extra.

Colours to own choice. With Coloured Bands if Required.

The 1938 'Langsett Lightweights' were the 'Austerfield' at 6 guineas (£6-6-0), the 'Laneham' at seven guineas, the 'Chesterfield' at eight guineas the 'Sheffield' at nine guineas, the 'Litchfield' at ten guineas, the 'Lincoln' at twelve guineas and the 'Track' at twelve guineas.

SHEFFIELD LANGSETT

A. M. CONTINENTAL

£12 - 5 - 0

FRAME. Built of Reynolds 531 Tubing. Size to Order. Chater-Lea Lugs Cut Out to exclusive design and neatly filed. Bracket Height 10¾ ins., Wheel Base 41½ ins. or to Order. Angles 73 head 71 seat tube or any Angles to Order. Chater-Lea Bottom Bracket and Head Parts.

FORKS. 531 Blades 7/8 in. to 5/8 in. Round. Continental Oval or to order. Chain and Seat Stays 531.

WHEELS. Dunlop High Pressure Rims. Size 26 ins. or 27 ins., B.W. Front Hub No. 6, ¼ in. bearings. Bonderised Black Enamelled Double Butted Spokes.

TYRES. Dunlop High Pressure, or if 26 Wheels are fitted, choice of Dunlop Sprite or John Bull Safety Speed.

TRANSMISSION. Williams C1,000 3 arm Lightweight.

SADDLE. B.17 standard. B.17N, B.17 flyer, or to order.

HANDLEBARS. To Order. Alloy Bend.

BRAKES. Continental " Lam " Alloy Front and Rear.

CHAIN. Elite.

PEDALS. Cyclo Lightweight or Light Continental.

MUDGUARDS. Bluemels White Featherweight with Reflector.

FINISH. Enamelled any Colour. Lined or Panelled to choice Chromium Plated Fork Crown.

GEAR. Sturmey-Archer A.M. 3 speed with trigger control.

BLUEMELS 15 in. x ¾ in. Pump, Oil Gun Lubrication Throughout. Tools.

The 1939 catalogue, other models included 'Continental Lichfield', 'Blyth', 'Lincoln', 'Selby', 'Ollerton', 'Derby' and 'Continental Laneham'.

THE "LANGSETT" LIGHTWEIGHT TENTS.

Suitable for cyclists or ramblers on account of their extreme lightness and the small space they take up when the tent, pegs and lines are packed away in the compact bag supplied with each tent.

Minor "W" white tent cloth ... . price 17/6
  „ "G" green Willesden proofed „ 24/6
  Size 6ft long, 4ft 3in wide, 3ft 6in high, 6in walls, weight 5½ lbs

Major "W" white tent cloth .... .. price 26/6
  „ "G" green Willesden proofed .. 35/6
  Size 7 ft long, 5 ft wide, 4 ft 6 in high, 1 ft walls, weight 6½ lbs.

Maximus "W" white tent cloth ... price 35/6
  „ "G" green Willesden proofed price 47/6
  Size 7ft long, 5 ft wide, 5ft 6 in high, 2 ft walls.

Ground Sheets, suitable for Minor 6 ft x 4 ft 5/6, Major or Maximus 7 ft x 5 ft 7/6, rubber proofed. All tents are fitted with three section poles with brass tube joints.

Quotations will be given for any type of tent on request.

Tents sent post free to any place in Great Britain.

Khaki Ruck-Sacks 15" x 17" **6/6.** 16" x 18" **7/6.** 1 pocket regulation design.
Khaki Shirts **4/11** and **5/11.** Black Shirts 5/6.
Khaki Shorts **2/11, 4/11** and **5/6.** Navy blue Shorts **4/11.**

Khaki and navy blue shorts are double seated. Suitable for cycling or rambling.

R. A. & E. S. SMITH, 64, LANGSETT ROAD, SHEFFIELD.
TELEPHONE 43401.

THE "LANGSETT" EASY-ACCESS TOURING BAG.

The "Langsett" Easy-Access Bag has been chiefly designed to make access to the bag a very simple matter. Before the "Langsett" bag was invented, access to a touring bag was often difficult. All cyclists are aware that the flap attached to the old type of bag (with the cape strapped on the top) fell over the opening of the bag when support was taken away. The flap of a "Langsett" bag is designed to fall towards the rear of the cycle and keep in place on its own, without being in the way. Bags strapped in the old manner sometimes caused articles to fall out. With a "Langsett" bag all difficulties have been over come, because it opens at the top near the saddle. The bag is easy to pack or unpack when attached to cycle, and carries its contents with safety.

Standard Tourer.
Size at top 5in wide 12in long, bottom 7in wide, 12in long, 9in deep, with two large side pockets, size over pockets 15½in, cape straps on top.

Low Saddle Bag.
Size at top 6in wide 13in long, bottom 9in wide 13in long 6in deep, with two large side pockets, same shape as bag. size over pockets 16½in, cape straps on top.

Special "Langsett" Easy-Access Bag.
With opening for mudguard clearance.

Size 6in wide, 9in deep, 14½in over pockets (opening approx. 3in deep at front) cape straps on top and fitted with two large side pockets. All the above bags can be fitted with special lock and key for 1/3 extra.

PRICES :—Khaki Twill 10/- each, Black Rexine 10/6 each, Black Pig Grain 16/6 each,
Registered Design Nos. 740,282, 752,723, 754,355. **Black Hide 17/6 each.** Post Free anywhere in Great Britain

Langsett Easy-Access bags can be made to special sizes to order.

The successful Langsett 'Easy-Access' touring bags were registered at the Patent Office in 1928.

TUBULAR TYRES AND RIMS.

WE ARE SHEFFIELD'S OFFICIAL SOLE AGENT FOR TABUCCHI SPECIALITIES

"CONSTRICTORS"

Silk Championship. Weighs 9½ oz. For cement tracks only ... ... **24/6** each

No. 1 Path Weighs 11½ oz. Suitable for all English tracks. ... ... **18/-** each

No. 2 Grass Weighs 13 oz. Thread **20/-** Silk Tubular **26/6** Skin Sides **1/6** extra

"Viper" Black fileband. Constrictor principle 26 or 27 Tread. ... ... **14/9** each

"Python" Red file tread, skin side free, 26 or 27 Thread 17 oz. (as illustrated) **17/6** each

No. 3 or "Adder" 17 oz. Thread **22/6** Silk Tubular **29/-** Skin Sides **1/6** extra

"Fifty" Fast Road Tyre 14½ oz. In file or smooth. Thread **21/-** Silk **27/6** Skin sides **1/6** extra.

"Asp" Tubular Super light 11 oz. Tyre Light Road **20/-** ... In Silk **26/6**

"CONSTRICTOR" Zone Sprint Tyres.
"Sewn up principle"

"Zone Light Path Racing" Suitable for good cement and indoor tracks. Cotton **17/-** 26, 6½ oz. in Silk **20/3** Also in 27 in.

"Zone Medium Path Racing" Suitable for track and short distance road work
26 x 1⅛, weighs 9 oz. in cotton **15/3**
26 x 1⅛, in silk 8 oz. **18/6**

"Zone Heavy Road" Wider file tread. Suitable all-round road work. 26 x 1⅛, weighs 12½ oz. 26 x 1⅛, weighs 11½ oz. in silk.
Cotton ... **16/6** Silk .. **19/9**
Skin sides **1/6** extra.

"Zone Light Road" Very popular, wide file band.
26 x 1⅛, weighs 15 oz. in cotton **17/-**
26 x 1⅛, weighs 10 oz. in silk **20/3**

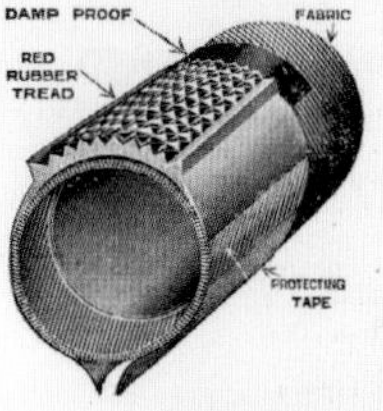

Illustrating Section of CONSTRICTOR PYTHON Tubular Tyre.

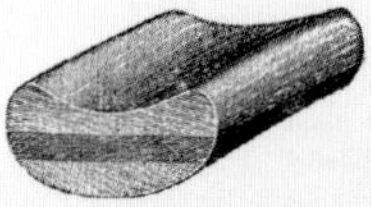

Tubular Rim Section.
CONSTRICTORS.

	per pair
Conloy Tubulars	**32/6**
Flat Maple	**25/-**
Flat Boa	**17/9**
Reinforced	**24/9**
Reinforced Boa	**17/3**
Boston (Maple)	**24/6**
Boston Boa (Maple)	**17/3**
Cobra Beachwood	**15/-**
"TABUCCHI'S"	
Italian Maple	**18/-**
Fiamme Tubular	**34/-**
"LANGSETT'S"	
Flat Maple	**15/6**

"DUNLOPS"

No.	Type of Tread	Weight	Actual Width Silk
1	Smooth	8¾ oz	1 1-32"
2	Smooth	9½ oz	1 1-16"
3	Fine File	12 oz	1 1-16"
4	Fine File	13 oz	1 1-16"
5	Smooth Centre	13 oz	1 1-16"
6	Heavy File	13¾ oz	1 1-16"
7	Heavy File	14 oz	1⅛"

Price **15/-** each Cotton.
„ **26/6** „ Silk.
Sizes · 26" and 27"

"TABUCCHIS"

"Tabucchi" No. 3 "All Rounder" Weight 12½ oz (approx.) 26 or 27 ... ... **15/-**

"Tabucchi" Olympic Grass Track. Bold file pattern, well down on sides 27 x 1⅛ only **20/-**

"Tabucchi" Super 50. Velvet black high carbon band. White Band if desired. 26 or 27 in. **19/6**

"Tabucchi Olympic Tubular. Made of English spun Egyptian Cotton, tough Para rubber Tread Weighs approx. 12 oz. 26 in. or 27 in. **20/-**

"Tabucchi Path" Internationally Famed. Weighs 7 oz. 27 x 1⅛ or 27 x 1 1-16 only **21/-**

"MERLINS"

Merlin Tubulars from **19/-** each

Constrictor Tubular Repair Outfits Large 1/- Small 6d. Constrictor Tacky Cement Tubes 6d. ¼ lb. 1/6

FULL RANGE OF CONSTRICTOR SPECIALITIES ALWAYS IN STOCK

WHEELS

Have your Wheels built by an expert Wheel Builder, not a piece-time worker trying to beat the clock. We guarantee all Wheels to be built in our own works by experienced mechanics, all Spokes are at correct tension to ensure liveliness. Only best Coventry Spokes are used.

1935 SPRINT BARGAIN OFFER. Built with Italian Flat Maple Rims, Bayliss-Wiley, Narrow Barrel Lightweight Racing Hubs (D.C. Rear), Black Butted Spokes 22/6 per pair.

SPECIAL OFFER

ENDRICK WHEELS 12/6 per pair. Built with black rims Bayliss-Wiley, chromium plated, narrow barrel, lightweight racing hubs, black spokes, rear double cog hubs.

SPECIAL OFFER

SPRINT WHEELS 27/6 per pair Built with Constrictor Boa Rims, Bayliss-Wiley, chromium plated, narrow barrel, lightweight racing hubs, black double butted spokes, rear double cog hub.

SPRINTS. Tied and Soldered 1/6 per pair.

HUBS Chromium plated unless otherwise stated. D.C. - Double Cog. S.C. - Single Cog.		**DUNLOP ENDRICK RIMS Black all over**			**CONSTICTOR SPRINT RIMS Boa or Cobra Beech**			**1st Quality Caminade Maple**		
		Front	Rear	Pair	Front	Rear	Pair	Front	Rear	Pair
Bayliss-Wiley Lightweight	D.C. Rear	6/6	7/6	13/6	14/-	15/-	27/6	19/-	20/-	37/6
Bayliss-Wiley Featherwei't 14½ oz.	D.C. „	12/-	13/6	25/-	18/-	19/6	37/-	23/-	24/6	47/-
Brampton Race	D.C. „	6/6	7/6	13/6	14/-	15/-	27/6	19/-	20/-	37/6
Blumfield 13½ oz. per pair	D.C. „	11/6	14/6	25/-	17/6	20/6	37/-	22/6	25/6	47/-
Tabucchi 12 oz per pair	D.C. „	Pairs	Only	31/-	—	—	43/-	—	—	53/-
Tabucchi 14 oz. per pair	D.C. „	Pairs	Only	26/6	—	—	38/6	—	—	48/6
B.S.A. Thin Barrel	S.C. or D.C. „	11/3	14/3	25/6	17/3	20/3	37/6	22/3	25/3	47/6
B.S.A. Standard	S.C. „	11/-	12/3	23/-	17/-	18/3	35/-	22/-	23/3	45/-
B.S.A. Standard	D.C. „	11/-	13/3	24/-	17/-	19/3	36/-	22/-	24/3	46/-
Constrictor, Light Steel	S.C. or D.C. „	11/-	14/3	25/-	17/-	20/3	37/-	22/-	25/3	47/-
Conloy	D.C. „	14/-	18/-	31/-	20/-	24/-	43/-	25/-	29/-	53/-
Boa, Nickel Plated	D.C. „	8/3	10/3	18/-	14/3	16/3	40/-	19/3	21/3	50/-
Chater Lea (Disc Adjusting)	S.C. „	10/6	12/9	23/-	16/6	18/9	35/-	21/6	23/9	45/-
Chater-Lea (Nickel Plated)	D.C. „	10/6	14/6	25/-	16/6	20/6	37/-	21/6	25/6	47/-
Sturmey-Archer 2 Speed		—	24/-	—	—	—	40/-	—	—	50/-
Sturmey-Archer 2 Speed with Hub Brake		—	32/-	—						
Sturmey-Archer Hub Brake		19/-	21/-	40/-						
Sturmey-Archer Standard 3 Speed		—	28/-	—						
Sturmey-Archer St'd'd 3 Sp'd with H'b Brake		—	36/6	—						
Sturmey-Archer Close & Medium Ratios 3 Sp'd		—	36/6	—						
Sturmey-Archer Ditto with Hub Brake		—	40/-	—						

Extras to above Black Endrick Rims. Chromium Plated, 2/9 perpair. Chromium, Black Centre 3/6 per pair. Wood Coloured, 3/0 per pair. "Tabucchi" W.O. Fiame 16 oz. 27/6 per pair. Constrictor W.O. Light Conloy 35/- per pair. Dunlop High Pressure Rims, 20 oz. lighter than Endrick, 5/- per pair (chromium finish).

Extras for Sprint Wheels.

If **Constrictor Conloy Rims** are required add **7/6** per pair on the 1st Quality Price.

For **Tabucchi Maple** add 3/6 per pair on the Constrictor Boa Quality Price.

For **Tabucchi Fiame** add 7/- per pair on to the Constrictor 1st Quality Price.

TANDEM WHEELS BUILT TO ORDER, - SEE GEAR PAGE IN THIS CATALOGUE.

Tyres and wheels as listed in the 1935 catalogue.

Roller competition at the Infirmary Road shop in 1936.
R.A. Smith is in front of the clock on the left,
E.S. Smith in front of the clock on the right.

ROLLER COMPETITION

TO BE HELD FROM
JANUARY 22nd, 1936
TO
FEBRUARY 1st, 1936
AT

R. A. & E. S. SMITH'S

184, 186, 188. INFIRMARY ROAD,
SHEFFIELD.

EVENTS.

Event 1 Lady's ¼ Mile Scratch Event.
  „   2 Gent's ¼ Mile Scratch Event.
  „   3   „   ½ Mile Scratch Event.

NOVICE EVENT.

  „   4 Gent's ¼ Mile Scratch Event.
Open to any rider who has not won a prize in any Open Event

YOUTH'S EVENT.

Event 5 Youth's ¼ Mile Scratch Event.
Open to any Youth under 16 Years.

OLDER RIDERS.

Event 6 Gent's ¼ Mile Scratch Event.
Open to Gent's over 35 Years.

CLUBMAN'S TEAM RACE.

Event 7 Gent's ¼ Mile Scratch Event.
4 Riders to form a Team. Each rider to ride for one Club only.
This rule of course applies to riders belonging to two or more
Clubs.

ENTRY FORMS.

These may be obtained through any Langsett Agent.
Langsett Branch or Head Office and Showrooms

Langsett Branches	Agent.	Agent.
53, West Street, Sheffield, 1.	Brompton Cycle Stores 416, Chatsworth Rd., Brompton,	Mr. Freeman, West St., Beighton.
64, Langsett Road, Sheffield, 6.	Chesterfield.	

Head badge
of the early 1930s

22

The 1950s – the new era

The connection with Rose Brothers led to the firm's occupation in 1951 of Wharncliffe Works at Green Lane, near the city centre end of Penistone Road. This was for the new engineering work and also provided a spacious frame building workshop with better facilities. The stove enamelled special finishes were done here in the paint finishing department, with the superb lining and hand paint finishes done by Les Lawson. The whole of the Infirmary Road premises then became the showroom, the dividing walls knocked through to make a row of five high quality interconnected shops, nicely decorated with excellent displays for cycles, accessories and also toys, including Meccano and Dinky.

Allan looked after the financial side of the business and ran the retail shops. His office was at the back of the Infirmary Road shops. Edward was in charge of the engineering orders and workshops, with his office at the Green Lane works. The West Street shop was closed in 1952, after surviving the Wartime bombing with only some stock damaged.

The Langsett framesets produced in the 1950s were of extremely high quality. Cycling enjoyed a new era with technical innovations after the War providing true 'lightweight' bicycles fitted with derailleur gears and aluminium alloy wheel rims, hubs, handlebars, brakes, etc. Road racing became popular and the Tour de France helped to make owning a competition bicycle fashionable. Reg Harris, a Lancashire clubman and silver medallist in the 1948 Olympics was Sportsman of the Year in 1950 and one of the best known personalities of the time. The 'road racing' specification (as opposed to 'track' or 'time trial' etc.) was the standard frame design and also known as 'massed start'; this was the model supplied to enthusiastic riders as well as the racing cyclists with mudguard eyes on the fork ends. The Langsett 'Professional' model, built to order with Reynolds 531 tubing and Nervex lugs was the pinnacle. The 'Conquest' was of the same high standard and specification but was not built to order and was made in small batches to be sold 'off the peg' and therefore less expensive than the Professional. Previously these had been known as the 'sixteen pounds nineteen and six' model and the 'twelve guinea' model. The 'Challenger' frameset and the 'Paramount' complete bicycle were the less expensive models supplied by other manufacturers to R.A. Smith's specification but not built in the Langsett workshop, the Langsett transfers applied after delivery. Every 'Professional' and 'Conquest' frameset was hand built in the Langsett workshop. At this time, Derek Morton, a skilled craftsman and engineer, was an important member of the team constructing the frames. In charge of the frameset order book was Arthur Davidson, a keen cyclist, at the Infirmary Road shop. He recorded all orders from 1952, listing the customer, frame size and colour. When ordered each frame was allocated a consecutive serial number, starting with the number 1 at the beginning of each year. This number was followed by the number of the month and the year – i.e. 14 3 53 = number 14 ordered March 1953. Initially in the order book there was a space between the numbers but in 1958 the spaces were omitted – 921058 = number 92 ordered October 1958. In addition some numbers had letter as a prefix. In 1952 'LM' (Langsett Morton), in February 1954 this was replaced by 'P' (Professional) or 'C' (Conquest). The prefix was dropped in 1958. The number was stamped beneath the bottom bracket on every frame, but it should be noted that the above details are as shown in the order book, and the spacing and prefix may not exactly correspond to the frame marking. Derek Morton left in 1959 to join Reg Harris and to set up the bicycle production at his factory. Later he was involved with my attempt to revive the Langsett Bicycle in 1974. The firm's stand at the York Cycle Rally in 1954 to 1958 showed the cycles to good advantage in the style of the time. One of the models made for the 1955 stand was a novelty miniature bicycle built on a 'Professional Junior' 16" frame. This is shown in the frameset record book as number P 45755 and enamelled ruby, although I remember this being yellow, probably re-finished for another display. Details of the curved rear brake bridge of the 'Professional' and the rear fork ends, both mounted on small plinths were also made. Also in 1955 the Tour of Britain was won by Tony Hewson with Dick Bartrop third, both riding Langsett 'Professional' cycles, and for the following years special transfers were applied to the seat tubes of Langsett framesets to commemorate this.

Roller competitions (where the bicycle is ridden on stationary rollers which measure the speed) had been held at the Infirmary Road shop in January 1936, and in February 1952 the Essoldo Cinema at Sheffield Lane Top was the venue for the Langsett roller racing competitions over six evenings.

R.A. Smith's 1930s design for the head transfer.
He drew the original artwork 12 inches wide.

AS USED IN THE TOUR OF BRITAIN

SPECIFICATION

Reynolds 531 Double Butted Tubing throughout.

Frame size and angles to your individual requirements.

Lugs neatly cut and filed.

531 Oval Round Fork Blades to our exclusive pattern.

531 Double Taper Seat Stays with extra-rigid bridge strengthened and drilled for rear brake.

531 Round Oval Round Chain Stays.

"Competition" type front and rear fork ends to your choice for Simplex or Benelux Gears. Finest quality Head and Bottom Bracket Fittings.

All fittings brazed on as required at no extra cost.

Finish; any colour to choice in Enamel, Flamboyant or Polychromatic.

Lugs picked out in contrasting colour, Double Box Lining, Head and Seat Tube panels as desired. Fork crown, chromed.

£16 - 19 - 6

The Sheffield Langsett 'Professional' frameset of 1955. Built in the Langsett workshop to individual specification with curved rear brake bridge and the Nervex lugs neatly cut and filed: finished in high quality stove enamel in the paint shop.

The first Langsett Road Race 1951, competitors are preparing to start at Infirmary Road.

THE SHEFFIELD PHOENIX ROAD CLUB

of the

BRITISH LEAGUE OF RACING CYCLISTS

Present, on behalf of

THE LANGSETT LIGHTWEIGHT CYCLES LTD.

(R. A. and E. S. SMITH)

182-192 Infirmary Road   53-55 West Street

Sheffield

THE

Langsett Lightweight Cycles

ROAD RACE

On SUNDAY, APRIL 22nd, 1951

Starting from **182-192 Infirmary Road** at 12 o'clock noon and finishing at **Malin Bridge** at approx. 3 p.m.

OFFICIALS

CHIEF JUDGE	**E. GILBERT**
TIMEKEEPER	**D. BARKER**
COMPETITORS' STEWARD	**K. WILLIS**
MACHINE EXAMINER	**K. SHAW**
EVENT ORGANISER	**Mr. R. BRAMHALL,**
	204a Chippinghouse Road, Sheffield

Changing Accommodation — Hillsborough Baths

COURSE

First Lap—
Infirmary Road, Malin Bridge, Rivelin Post Office, Ladybower, Bamford, Hathersage, Burbage Moor (Prime), Ringinglow, Lodge Moor, Crosspool, Rivelin Post Office.

Second Lap—
Ladybower, Bamford, Hathersage, Burbage Moor (Prime), Ringinglow, Lodge Moor, Crosspool, Rivelin Post Office, Malin Bridge.

DISTANCE — 52 Miles (approx.)

● *Will Spectators kindly assist by KEEPING OFF THE ROAD, particularly at the Finish. Thank you*

COMPETITORS

No.	Name	Club	Notable Performance	
1	N. Taylor	Sheffield Phoenix	1st N. Mid. Sect. Champs.	1950
2	J. Pound	R.C. ('A' Team)	1st Bollington R.R.	1950
3	L. Wakelam	do.	3rd Mercury T.T.	1951
4	S. Wilson	do.	2nd Mercury T.T.	1951
5	R. Parkin	Bradford R.C.C.	1st National Am. Champs.	1950
6	P. Tesseyman	do.	1st Yorks. Plains R.R.	1950
7	J. Sharp	do.		
8	B. Lowde	do.		
9	K. Slater	Sheffield R.C.C.	4th Burbage Circuit R.R.	1950
10	K. Barden	do.	5th Bollington R.R.	1950
11	G. Derby	do.	1st Ripley R.R.	1950
12	P. Raw	do.	5th Handleys R.R.	1950
13	H. Martin	Sheffield Phoenix	1st Woodboro' Hill R.R.	1950
14	E. Hook	R.C. ('B' Team)	3rd Macclesfield R.R.	1950
15	D. Morton	do.	3rd Woodboro' Hill R.R.	1950
16	P. Newbold	do.	4th R.A.F. Champs.	1949
17	N. Inman	S. Manchester R.C.C.	1st Bowland R.R.	1950
18	T. Williams	do.		
19	E. Sandbach	do.		
20	R. Johnson	do.	2nd Glossop Velo. R.R.	1950
21	W. Hall	Sheffield Phoenix		
22	W. Tomlinson	R.C. ('C' Team)		
23	K. Wood	do.		
24	T. Thornton	do.		
25	J. Hibell	Birmingham Pr. R.C.	1st Norfolk G.P.	1950
26	M. Varley	do.	1st North Liverpool R.R.	1950
27	P. Hall	do.	2nd Stonebridge T.T.T.	1950
28	G. Roberts	Wolverhampton W.		
29	W. Craig	Notts. Olympic R.C.	2nd Chevin R.R.	1951
30	G. Taylor	Birmingham Olym.	4th Nuneaton G.P.	1950
31	C. Watts	do.		
32	D. Cowell	do.		
33	F. Saynor	Sheffield Merc. R.C.		
34	L. Saynor	do.		
35	E. Connah	Sheffield Phoenix	5th N. Mids. Jun. Champs.	1950
36	D. Midgley	R.C.		
37	K. Smith	do.		
38	R. Barratt	Sheffield R.C.C.		
39	J. Rowan	do.		
40	P. McFarlane	do.	2nd Pennine Valley G.P.	1950
		Reserves		
41	A. Ward	Sheffield Phoenix R.C.		
42	K. Bramhall	do.		

PRIZES

1st   Value £3 and a **Benelux Change Speed Gear.**
2nd   Value £2 and a **Pair of Fleming Cycling Shoes.**
3rd   Value £1 and a **Pair of Mobbs Cycling Shoes.**
4th   Value 10/-

Team (3 Riders)—
3 Pairs of Bailey Mudguards and 3 Apex Inflators.
1st   Prime   Value 10/-
2nd   Prime   Value 10/-

The Langsett Cycles Road Race 1951-1967

The first Langsett Lightweight Cycles Road race was on Sunday, 22nd April 1951. In conjunction with the Sheffield Phoenix Road Club and under British League of Racing Cyclists rules, it was regarded as one of the toughest single stage road races and a popular event until 1967. The 1951 course of 52 miles started at the Infirmary Road shop, neutralised to Malin Bridge, then two laps of a circuit through Rivelin, Bamford, Hathersage, Ringinglow and return to Malin Bridge for the finish.

The second race in 1952 had five laps of a 10 mile circuit to start and finish at Loxley Road, through Dungworth, Storrs and Low Bradfield. 1953 was the 90 mile course which was the basis for subsequent races up to 1962. Starting at the Infirmary Road shop, neutralised to Rivelin Valley, and then Bamford, Mam Tor, Chapel, Glossop, Snake Pass to Bamford, and then two laps of the second circuit through Hathersage and Moscar to finish at Rivelin, or Moscar Top from 1954. In 1955 appalling weather developed soon after the race began and the 90 mile race was reduced to 55 miles: rain, hail, heavy snow and cold temperatures resulted in only seven of the thirty-two starters finishing the course. The race winner was Graham Vines (2 hrs 47 min), L. Gill second and K. Russell third. In 1960, the 90 mile course consisted of two laps of a circuit from Rivelin Valley Road to Moscar, Bamford, Hathersage, Ringinglow, Rivelin, and then one lap of a second circuit: Bamford, Mam Tor, Chapel, Glossop, Snake Pass, Moscar, to finish near the Bell Hagg Inn. The 1961 and 1962 races were the same course but with just one lap of the first circuit and a total of 70 miles. The 1963 race was moved to Wentworth, starting and finishing at West Melton: 12 laps through Wentworth and Stubbin. From 1964 to 1967 the same course was reduced to 10 laps.

The 'Vulcan' trophy, a replica of the statue mounted on the pinnacle of the Sheffield town hall, was awarded annually to the winner to be held for one year:

1951	R. Johnson	1957	R. Coe
1952	J. Pottier	1958	I. Sandbach
1953	R. Maitland	1959	J. Geddes
1954	A. Isley	1960	G. Taylor
1955	G. Vines	1961	R. Coe
1956	T. Hallam	1962	J. Macklam

1957 saw the Langsett Road Race Team, with additional sponsorship by 'The Racing Cyclist Journal', the team riders were Pete Ryalls, Alan Hoyland, H. Gould, Dave Orford, Brian Trippett and John Bennett. The 1958 team included George Shaw and the team had additional 'Ovaltine' sponsorship.

Around the time of the race a model of the course was displayed in the shop window, with miniature cyclists and showing the main features; the earlier tradition of interesting window displays was evident throughout the post-war period. Other things seen in the windows included a cycling photographic competition in 1950, with sections for racing, touring, and club life.

The 1951 Langsett Cycles Road race leaving on Infirmary Road.

The Langsett Lightweight Cycles Road Races
1951 to 1967.

Cutthroat bridge on the fast descent from Moscar to Ladybower.

The 1958 Langsett Cycles Road Race Team.
Dave Orford   Alan Hoyland   George Shaw   Pete Ryalls   Brian Trippett   Johnny Bennet

LANGSETT LIGHTWEIGHT CYCLES

FOURTH ANNUAL ROAD RACE

DISTANCE **90** MILES

A SHEFFIELD PHŒNIX C. C. PROMOTION
Under B.L.R.C. Rules

THE VULCAN TROPHY
Awarded annually to the winner of the race.

SUNDAY MAY 30th. 1954

Starting from Langsett Lightweight Cycles Ltd.,
182 - 192 Infirmary Road at 10 - 30 a. m.

OFFICIAL PROGRAMME ———————————— GRATIS
(With the Compliments of Langsett Lightweight Cycles Ltd).

OFFICIALS

Director of the Course	.. ..	E. Gilbert
Timekeeper	.. ..	H. Cutler
Chief Judges	.. ..	Messrs J Needham & K. Shaw
Prime Judges	..	Messrs B. Clayton, J. Rowan & K. Slater
Machine Examiner	.. .. ..	K. Oxley
Competitors Steward	.. ..	K. Willis
Mobile Marshals	Messrs. P. Newbould, D. Morton, L. Dodd & W. Day	

EVENT ORGANISER Roy F. Bramhall, c/o Langsett Lightweight Cycles Ltd
to whom all complaints regarding the race, should be made in writing.

EVENT HEADQUARTERS & CHANGING ACCOMODATION:
Hillsborough Baths, Langsett Road, Sheffield 6.
(all motor vehicles **MUST** be parked off the main road).

THE COURSE

Start outside the premises of Langsett Lightweight Cycles Ltd., neutralised to Rivelin Valley Road, Moscar, left to Bamford, left at "The Marquis of Granby", Hathersage. Burbage PRIME, left at Ringinglow, Lodge Moor, Coldwell Lane, (halt), Rivelin Post Office, Moscar, left to Bamford, right at "The Marquis of Granby", Castelton, **(beware bad bends)**, Mam Tor PRIME, Sparrow-Pit, Chapel **(caution needed)**, Hayfield, Chunnell, **(dangerous decent)**, Glossop, Turn right at lights, Snake PRIME, Lady Bower, Turn right to Bamford, left at "The Marquis of Granby", Hathersage, Burbage PRIME, left at Ringinglow, Lodge Moor, Coldwell Lane, **(halt)**, Rivelin Post Office, (4 miles to go). Continue up Manchester Road, to the FINISH at Moscar Top.

APPROX. TIME OF FINISH 2-45 p.m.

PRIZE LIST

1st.		£10 - 10 - 0
also the Vulcan Trophy to be held for one year.		
2nd.		£ 5 - 5 - 0
3rd.		£ 4 - 4 - 0
4th.		£ 3 - 3 - 0
5th.		£ 2 - 2 - 0
6th.		£ 1 - 10 - 0
7th.		£ 1 - 0 - 0

TEAM PRIZE

1st. Team of 3 riders	£ 6 - 0 - 0
2nd. Team of 3 riders	£ 3 - 3 - 0
3rd. Team of 3 riders	£ 2 - 5 - 0

SPECIAL PRIZE

King of the Mountains	£ 4 - 4 - 0

HIDDEN PRIME AWARDS

1st. Prime	1. Hutchinson Tubular
2nd. Prime	1. Hutchinson Tubular

Kindly Donated by Messrs. Hutchinson Ltd.

COMPETITORS

No.	Name	Notable Performance	Club/Sponsor
1.	R. Maitland	National Independent Champion	B. S. A. Cycles
2.	S. Jones	1st. Dover-London R.R. 1953	,,
3.	A. Ilsley	2nd. Elmsall Spring Classic 1954	,,
4.	P. Pryor	1st. Three Sister Cities, Antwerp 1953	,,
5.	L. Wilton	2nd. Gresley Memorial R.R. 1954	,,
6.	A. Newman	1st. les Adams Memorial R.R. 1953	,,
7.	L. Scales	2nd. Tour of Britain 1952-53	Wearwell Cycles
8.	J. Pottier	3rd. Tour of Britain 1953	,,
9.	J. Welch	Member of 1st. Team, Tour of Britain 1953	,,
10.	I. Greenfield	1st. "Substitute" R R. 1954	,,
11	T. Fenwick	1st. London-Battle R.R. 1953	,,
12.	K. Mitchell	2nd. "Substitute" R R. 1954	,,
13.	D. Bedwell	3rd. Tour of Calvados, France 1954	Hercules Cycles
14	K. Joy	3rd. Elmsall Spring Classic 1954	,,
15.	C. Parker	1st. Dover-London R.R. 1954	,,
16.	D. Talbot	1st. Elmsall Spring Classic 1954	,,
17.	F. Krebs	1st. Tour of the Chilterns 1953	,,
18.	D. Buttle	3rd. V-C. Calvados, France 1953	,,
19.	I. Steel	1st. Warsaw-Berlin-Prague 1953	Viking Cycles
20.	F. Seel	1st. Tour of the Chase 1951	,,
21.	B. Wood	3rd. Tour of Mexico 1953	,,
22.	D. Booker	1st. Gresley Memorial R R. 1954	,,
23.	A. Ashmore	2nd. Midland Grand Prix 1953	,,
24.	K. Jowett	1st. Tour of the Peaks 1953	,,
25.	K. Russell	1st. Tour of Britain 1952	Ellis-Briggs Cycles
26.	F. Nichols	1st. Tour of the Cotswolds 1952	,,
27.	B. Robinson	2nd. Tour of the Chilterns 1953	,,
28.	P. Southart	1st. Coast to Coast R R. 1953	Pennine Cycles
29.	R. Parkin	2nd. Border Grand Prix 1953	,,
30.	B. Packer	1st. Coronation R.R. 1953	Unsponsored
31	D. Wilson	1st. Anniversary R.R. 1953	Gnutti Accessories
32.	D. Robinson	1st. Amateur Tour of Britain 1952	,,
33.	L. Wade	1st. Notts Skegness 1952	,,
34.	A. Taylor	2nd. Tour of Britain 1951	Wilson Cycles
35.	S. Wilson	1st. Mercury R.R. 1953	,,
36.	D. Orford	1st. Students Union R.R. 1953	,,
37.	D Petty	1st. Blyth R.R. 1953	,,
38.	I. Brown	3rd. Aspirant, Tour of Britain 1953	Unsponsored

COMPETITORS

No.	Name	Notable Performance	Club/Category
1	G. Vines	1st. Langsett R.R. 1955	London/Ind.
2	L. J. Scales	1st. London-Holyhead R.R. '51	London/Ind.
3	K. Mitchell	Tour de France, 1955.	London/Ind.
4	D. Bedwell	1st. Bournemouth 3 Day '56	London/Ind.
5	B. Wood	3rd. Tour of Mexico, 1953	Bev Wood Cycles/Ind.
6	K. Stratford	1st. Wilsden Gala R.R. 1955.	Lune R. C. /Ind
7	K. Jowett	1st. Dunsmoor R.R. 1955.	Independent.
8	R. J. Maitland	1st. Langsett R.R. 1953	Concorde R.C./Ind.
9	A. Ilsley	Pro/Ind. Champion 1954.	Concorde R.C./Ind.
10	S. Jones	1st. Gresley Mem. R.R. 1955	Concorde R.C./Ind.
11	D. Petty	2nd. Charnwood Forest R.R. '55	Independent
12	T. Fenwick	1st. Dover-London R.R. '55	Trev. Fenwick Cycles
13	J. H. Swinney	1st. Exeter R.R. 1955.	Exe Valley R.C./Ind.
14	J. F. Wilson	Tour of Yugoslavia, 1955	Wilson Cycles/Ind.
15	S. Wilson	1st. City Road Race, 1953	Wilson Cycles/Ind.
16	M. Hinch	2nd. East Coast R.R. 1955	Wilson Cycles/Ind.
17	J. Andrews	1st. Nth. London Champs. 1955	London Aspirant
18	J. Morris	1st. Chequers G.P. 1955	London Aspirant
19	I. Barrett	1st. Sth. London Champs.1955	London Aspirant
20	D. Blissett	1st. Castlenau R.R. 1955	London Aspirant
21	R. Wallman	2nd. Atlas 3 Day R.R. 1956	Domino Road Club
22	R. Taylor	1st. West Command R.R. 1955	Domino Road Club
23	A. Hope	1st. Widnes Grand Prix 1956	Domino Road Club
24	R. Johnson	1st. Langsett R.R. 1955	Tame Valley R.C.
25	A. Keenhan	2nd. Tour of Hanchurch. '55	Tame Valley R.C.
26	T. Knox	2nd. Tour of the Roaches. '55	Tame Valley R.C.
27	N. Storey	2nd. Nth. Staffs G.P. 1955	Tame Valley R.C.
28	B. Haskell	1st. Tour of the Border. 1956	Huddersfield R.C.
29	E. Penrose	1st. Tame Valley R.R. 1949	Huddersfield R.C.
30	D. Robinson	National Amateur Champ. 1955	Huddersfield R.C.
31	J. Short	1st. Spring Criterium. 1956	Falcon R.C.
32	P. McFarlane	2nd. Anniversary R.R. 1955	Falcon R.C.
33	A. Huntingdon	2nd. St. Leger R.R. 1955	Falcon R.C.
34	D. Midgley	2nd. Greenmoor R.R. 1955	Falcon R.C.
35	E. Wren	2nd. Mallerstang R.R. 1955	Falcon R.C.
36	P. Nowell	1st. Holcombe Cir. R.R. 1949	Lune R.C.Z.
37	T. Hallam	2nd. Nidderdale R.R. 1955	City R.C.
38	T. Lloyd	3rd. Chivenor Cir. R.R. 1955.	Coventry Three Spires R.C.
39	J. L. Gill	2nd. Langsett R.R. 1956	Coventry Three Spires R.C.
40	H. Bamforth	1st. Moorside G.P. 1954	Saddleworth Border R.C.
41	A. Connolly	3rd. Farnley R.R. 1955	Oldham Meteor R.C.
42	A. Hoyland	2nd. Autumn R.R. 1955	Atlas R.C.
43	K. Lyne	2nd. Burbage R.R. 1955	Atlas R.C.
44	P. A. Ryalls	2nd. St. Leger R.R. 1955	Atlas R.C.
45	J. W. Hepworth	4th. Cir. of the Handleys. '55.	Atlas R.C.
46	R. Bartrop	3rd. Tour of Britain 1955	Falcon R.C.

1956 Race competitors.

OFFICIAL INSTRUCTIONS

RIDERS:— Machines must be examined before 10 a.m.
From the start the competitors will ride in an orderly manner 50 yards behind the Director's car, until the de-neutralisation signal is given.
The Highway Code must be strictly observed and all Police and Marshal's instructions carried out immediately.

FOLLOWING CARS etc:— On no account will any trade vehicle be allowed to overtake the peloton without permission from the Director.

PLEASE PARK ALL VEHICLES ACCORDING TO THE MARSHAL'S INSTRUCTIONS IN ORDER TO AVOID CONGESTION OF THE ROAD AT THE FINISH.

1954 Langsett Cycles Road Race programme.

The 1955 Langsett Cycles Road Race leaving Infirmary Road behind the race director's car. The 90 mile race distance was reduced to 55 miles because of the extremely bad weather, with only 7 of the 32 starters completeing the course.

COMPETITORS - LANGSETT ROAD RACE 1958

1	R. Coe (1st 1957)	Elswick/Hopper Cycles
2	S. Wilson	"
3	A. Blaydon	"
4	F. Clements	"
5	H. Reynolds	"
6	P. Ryalls	Ovaltine/Langsett Cycles
7	A. Hoyland	"
8	G. Shaw	"
9	D. Orford	"
10	B. Trippett	"
11	J. Bennett	"
12	B. Haskell (3rd 1957)	Viking Cycles
13	D. Bartrop (2nd 1957)	"
14	T. Oldfield	"
15	L. Gill (2nd 1955 & 1956)	"
16	B. Eastwood	"
17	T. Penvose	"
18	K. Stratford	Wilson Cycles
19	D. Petty	"
20	P. Nowell	"
21	B. Clayton	Thompson Cycles
22	B. Finney	"
23	A. Lyne	"
24	A. Doyle	"
25	A. Williamson	Racing Cyclists Journal/Wearwell
26	I. Sharp	"
27	A. Kennahan	"
28	R. Levers	Sheffield Phoenix C.C.
29	P. Hampson	"
30	J. Clayton	Glossop Velo R.C.
31	C. Sparkes	Birmingham Premier R.C.
32	G. Hamilton	"
33	G. Foster	"
34	B. Bodenham	"
35	J. Parker	"
36	B. Maitland (1st 1956)	Ilsley/Maitland Cycles
37	A. Ilsley (1st 1954)	"
38	S. Jones (3rd 1956)	"
39	I. Sandbach	South Pennine Coureurs
40	K. Jowett (2nd 1953)	Pennine Cycles
41	K. Jowett	"
42	N. Storey	Bev Wood Cycles/Silkin
43	N. Magee	"
44	P. Street	"
45	A. Hope	"
46	A. McPherson	Johnstone Wheelers (S.C.U.)
47	P. McFarlane	Falcon R.C.
48	D. Midgeley	"
49	A. Huntingdon	"
50	T. Mayfield	Manchester Velo Club
51	F. Evans	"
52	F. Garvey	"
53	P. Wilson	"
54	F. Hodgins	"
55	T. Hallam (1st 1956)	Sheffield City R.C.
56	P. Ellison	Ellis Briggs Cycles
57	P. R. Ward	Ribble Valley C.R.C.

1958 Race competitors.

COMPETITORS

1	T. Hallam	...	1st, Langsett R.R., 1956	...	...	Sheffield City R.C.
2	D. Bedwell	...	1st, Bournemouth 3 days, 1956			Rory O'Brien/Simplex
3	J. Morris	...	1st, Thornhill Classic, 1956	...	...	Wally Green Cycles
4	J. Swinney	...	1st, Exeter R.R., 1955	...	...	Meridian Cycles
5	I. Brown	...	16th, Tour of Champagne, 1957	...	...	Hill Special Cycles
6	J. Andrews	...	1st, North London Champs., 1955	...	...	Fred Dean Cycles
7	K. Jowett	...	1st, Buxton Spring R.R.,1957...	...	...	Pennine Cycles
8	P. Ellison	...	1st, Telegraph-Argus 3 day,1955		...	Pennine Cycles
9	R. Maitland	...	1st, Gresley Memorial R.R., 1957			Ilsley-Maitland Cycles
10	S. Jones	...	1st, Gresley Memorial R.R., 1956		...	Ilsley-Maitland Cycles
11	A. Ilsley	...	1st, South Elmsall R.R.,1957	...	...	Ilsley-Maitland Cycles
12	P. Street	...	2nd, Macclesfield G.P., 1956	...	...	Bev Wood-Silkin
13	R. Magee	...	1st, Holcombe Cir. R.R., 1956		...	Bev Wood-Silkin
14	A. Hope	...	1st,Widnes G.P., 1956 ...	...	...	Bev Wood-Silkin
15	D. Blissett	...	1st, Castlenau R.R., 1956	...	...	Whitcomb Trading Co.
16	D. Hutton	...	1st, Annual Circuit R.R., 1957			Whitcomb Trading Co.
17	R. Beck	...	1st, Dover—London, 1957	...	...	Whitcomb Trading Co.
18	D. Sutherland	...	2nd, Annual Circuit R.R., 1957			Whitcomb Trading Co.
19	P. Hampson	...	1st, Hassop R.R., 1954...	...	...	Thompson Cycles
20	B. Finney	...	1st, Autumn R.R., 1955	...	...	Thompson Cycles
21	B. Clayton	...	2nd, Burbage R.R., 1955	...	...	Thompson Cycles
22	G. Vines	...	1st, Huddersfield R.R., 1957	...	...	Raxar-Fenwick
23	T. Fenwick	...	1st, Dover—London, 1956	...	...	Raxar-Fenwick
24	B.Hier	...	1st, Weston Grand Prix, 1956	...	...	Raxar-Fenwick
25	R. Sunderland	...	1st, Three Shires R.R., 1956	...	...	Raxar-Fenwick
26	B. Haskell	...	1st, Tour of Ireland, 1953 and 1955	...	...	Viking Cycles
27	E. Penvose	...	1st, Yorkshire Champs., 1956...	...	...	Viking Cycles
28	R. Bartrop	...	3rd, Tour of Britain, 1955	...	...	Viking Cycles
29	L. Gill	...	1st, Gresley Memorial R.R., 1953		...	Viking Cycles
30	T. Oldfield	...	1st, Tour of the Lakes, 1956	...	...	Viking Cycles
31	R. Eastwood	...	1st, Yorkshire Champs., 1955...	...	...	Viking Cycles
32	J. Wilson	...	Tour of Yugoslavia, 1955	...	...	Wilson Cycles
33	R. Coe	...	1st, Atlas Kermesse, 1957	...	...	Wilson Cycles
34	S. Wilson	...	3rd, Gresley Memorial R.R., 1957	...	...	Wilson Cycles
35	D. Petty	...	2nd, Charnwood Forest R.R., 1955	...	...	Wilson Cycles
36	K. Stratford	...	1st, Buxton Spring Classic, 1956	...	...	Wilson Cycles
37	T. Hewson	...	2nd, Grand Prix Zele, Belgium, 1957		Independent/Falcon R.C.
38	P. McFarlane	...	1st, Mercury R.R., 1956	...	...	Sheffield Falcon R.C.
39	D. Midgley	...	2nd, Greenmoor R.R., 1954	...	...	Sheffield Falcon R.C.
40	A. Huntingdon	...	2nd, North Derbyshire R.R., 1954	...	Sheffield Falcon R.C.
41	E. Wren	...	2nd, Mallerstang R.R., 1955	...	...	Sheffield Falcon R.C.
42	T. Mayfield	...	1st, Scunthorpe R.R., 1955	...	...	Sheffield Falcon R.C.
43	A. Hoyland	...	3rd, Cleethorpes Pursuit, 1957	...	Racing Cyclist Journal
44	P. Ryalls	...	2nd, St. Leger R.R., 1956	...	...	Racing Cyclist Journal
45	B. Trippett	...	2nd, East Pennine G.P., 1956 ...	...	Racing Cyclist Journal
46	D. Orford	...	1st, Circuit des Grimpeurs, 1957	...	Racing Cyclist Journal
47	J. Bennett	...	12th, Criterium Champs., 1956	...	Racing Cyclist Journal
48	H. Gould	...	5th, Criterium Champs., 1956	...	Racing Cyclist Journal
49	M. Hinch	...	2nd, East Coast R.R., 1956	...	...	Alp Cycles

1957 Race competitors.

"LANGSETT" LIGHTWEIGHT OILSKINS.

(FULLY GUARANTEED FOR 12 MONTHS)

"Langsett"
"Lightskin" Cape.

Extra light Oilskin, black, gold or dark green, length from top of collar : 42in front, and 39in back, length round skirt 118in full.

Price 9/11 each.

Special line—
Black Oilskin Cape 8/11
Length 42in.

"Langsett"
"Lightskin" Leggings.

Fitted with Patent Fastenings, 4 sizes, short medium, long and extra long, Black and gold.

Price 9/6 per pair.
Black oilskin leggings from 5/11 per pair.

Holdsworth's Oilskins.
Black or gold.

Goldskin Standard Cape 42in 12/6. Goldskin Sixfooter Cape 45in 16/-. Goldskin Koolah Cape 42in 15/6. Goldskin Sixfooter Cape 45in 13/6,

Saxon Oilskins.
Black or khaki. Saxon standard cape 39in
Price 12/- each.

"Langsett"
"Lightskin Six Footer". Cape.

Extra light Oilskin, black, gold or dark green, length from top of collar 45in front, and 42in back, length round skirt 142in full.

Price 11/6 each.

"Langsett"
"Lightskin" Sou'westers.

Lined with special cellular material to allow free circulation of air, this prevents moisture adhering to the head. Black, gold and green. Sizes 6¾, 6⅞, 7 and 7¼.

Price 3/6 each.

Paget Oilskins.

Black or khaki. Paget standard cape 42in. button neck.

Price 12/6 each.

Capes fitted with velvet collar, strap and buckle, weather proof "V" neck, capes black 36in 13/6, 39in 14/6, 42in 15/6, capes khaki 36in. 15/-, 39in 16/-, 42in 17/-,
Leggings, patent fastenings, black **9/6** khaki **11/6.**

OILSKINS SENT POST FREE.

RACING CLOTHING.

ALPACA JACKETS
Very Smart Cut.

SPECIAL OFFER.—Having had a large number of jackets cut to our usual style, made from a good quality black cloth, we are able to offer them at this very low price—**5/11 each.** Made in all sizes.

Jackets made from Strong Black Cotton   8/11 each.
     „   „   „   Fine   „   „   10/6   „
     „   „   „   „   „ Alpaca 12/6   „
     „   „   „   „ Grey   „ 12/6   „
Chest sizes 30, 32, 34, 36, 38, 40 and 42 inch. 6d extra for 44, 46 and 48 inch sizes. Alpacas made to special order.

RACING TIGHTS

Specially made to our cutting by a firm specializing in sports wear. All are fitted with double seat.

Special offer   Black Cotton 2/11   Good quality Black Cotton 3/9 per pair
Best quality   „   „   5/6   Cashmere all wool finest quality 10/6 „ „
     Sizes inside leg lengths 28, 30 and 32 in. waist 32, 34 and 36 in.

JERSEYS

High neck, 5 buttons on neck and shoulder, long sleeves rib neck and cuffs, made from black cotton 3/9 each. Roll collar, grey all wool Sweaters 7/11 each. Roll collar grey, best quality worsted heavy close knit 9/11 each.

PATH SHORTS
Special quality 1/6 pair. Black cotton double seated 2/6 and 3/9 per pair.

SKULL CAPS
Black cotton   1/- each.
Black cashmere 1/3 each.

Oilskins and clothing from the 1931 catalogue.

The end of the road

The 1960s saw a swift and dramatic slump in the cycle industry. The sales record book shows nine Langsett numbered framesets sold in 1952 and in 1953 eighty-one ordered and sold. 103 in 1954, 82 in 1955, 110 in 1956, 95 in 1957, 100 in 1958, 100 in 1959, 90 in 1960, 53 in 1961, 46 in 1962, 2 in 1963, and a single frame in 1964. Sales of specialist cycles at the Infirmary Road shop were greatly reduced and, sadly, the last true 'Sheffield Langsett' bicycle was sold in 1964. The building of the framesets had been found to be no longer economical. The final four frames were, in fact, made by Pennine Cycles. Increasingly poor trading figures resulted in the retail side of the business, which was the Infirmary Road shop, being sold to Mr. L. Taylor in 1968, with the Smith family having no further connection since that time. The engineering side of the business continued at Wharncliffe Works on Green Lane until 1976.

The short-lived new Sheffield Langsett

In 1977 I endeavoured to revive the Sheffield Langsett bicycle. My friend, Derek Morton (who built Langsett frames in the 1950s), was building his own excellent 'Morton' frames in limited numbers. I discussed my ideas with him and he produced several prototypes of our proposed designs for me. Derek's skills and long experience with cycles enabled him to make valuable contributions to my designs and plans for production. The production frames were to be made to the highest standards of construction and finish, using traditional methods and reflecting the original frames made in the 1950s and using Reynolds '531' tubing. The idea was to avoid 'bespoke' orders, and to manufacture and finish a small quantity of each size at one time; there were a limited number of sizes and all enamelled black with gold transfers. In this way the price could be kept within reasonable limits and thus would encourage sales of sufficient quantities to make the production viable. As these new cycle frames were to be made in Sheffield, it seemed appropriate for each frame to have a sterling silver head badge, hallmarked at the Sheffield Assay Office with the Marks for Sheffield and the year. The badge would be engraved with the owner's monogram. To protect the name 'Langsett', I registered it at the Patent Office as a trademark.

The new frames were very well received at the 1977 Harrogate International Cycle Show when we showed three prototype frames on our stand; one of these was displayed as bare metal without enamel to show the standard of workmanship. It was a very useful exercise to present them to cyclists and to assess the commercial prospects. In 1978 I exhibited at Harrogate again, enquiries and orders coming from all parts of the country and America. Unfortunately the venture did not succeed; I did not have sufficient finance or the sales facilities and structure to provide a proper service to customers. We did manage to make a number of frames to fulfil the orders I had taken at the shows, but much more investment would have been required to continue. Tragically Derek had become terminally ill, and I realised that my original ambition was no longer a possibility.

Stuart Smith's Sheffield Langsett 1977-1978 frames with the Sheffield hallmarked sterling silver head badge.

'My Cycling Life 1874-1947' by Herbert Smith

In 1947 Herbert Smith wrote this account of his cycling experiences.

(I have made only minor corrections and amendments and added some notes in brackets. The ordinary bicycle is, of course a, 'penny-farthing', which he also calls his 'spider wheel'.)

In my 20th year I rode to Boston in a day on an Ordinary Bicycle. In my 63rd year I rode to John O'Groats, over 1,000 miles in 15 days.

In 1874 when I was eight years of age I had my first ride on a wheel. In Edward Street a roundabout made from old wheels of all sizes and poles from a centre hub with platform. A man six feet tall stood with whip cracking and a lad turning the organ handle. We lads pushed the poles and the riders tried to pedal. Sometimes we got a ride and sometimes the whip! When I was 10 years old Bob Gregory lifted me onto his Boneshaker. Bob Gregory played football with Cleggs for Sheffield Club. After that short ride it made me long for a Spider Wheel, and I got my first mount in 1883. My mother said I must not buy one, but when I wheeled it home she did not turn me out, but a big thing it looked in the house. Bought it from Pashley, London Road. He sold me one that was two inches too large for me, and it had over one inch front rake on the forks. It was a second-hand old racer. I soon rode it on the flat, but downhill I lost the pedals.

Riding the ordinary

I had some good pals. My first go was for Ashopton. I walked to Crosspool and called at a blacksmith's shop to have my crank fastened on. He put me a red-hot wedge in and said that's alright sonny. Then I rode to Rivelin post office, and walked to Moscar top. Pals waited for me and lifted me on, but soon afterwards they had to jump off their cycles to stop me running away down the hill. Walked to Ashopton. Had a good time bird nesting and a tea for fourpence – cake, brown bread, one egg, butter and cream. Walked up to Ladybower and they lifted me on my machine.

Over the front I go, my bird eggs in my hat broken. The spring from the well at Ladybower came in handy, letting the water wash my head while my pals picked the shells off. Walked to Moscar top, rode to Rivelin post office and then walked home, my first outing with our new club.

My next ride was by myself, but I could get on now by jumping from the step onto the saddle, so I could go out for a ride. Going down Brocco Bank the machine was getting the master of me – put brake on – locked front wheel and sent me over the front. Picked myself up and walked through Hunter's Toll Bar up to Ecclesall church. Got on downhill, run away so went up Psalter Lane. Went just over the top of the hill and my hat blew off, could not stop until the bottom – had to walk back up the hill for it. The following ride was on Abbeydale Road through the old toll bar. When I was turning to go down for Little London a man got in front of me, my arms went round his neck and we both finished on the road together looking at each other. He was a good sort, he laughed and lifted me back on. I rode down to the railway bridge, caught the wall trying to turn and it threw me into the river, but I was nearly dry when I got home.

For my next ride I met a pal at Hunter's Bar to go to Grindleford. My saddle was very small with a three inch point, this caught in a hole in my pants and down I came, ripping both of the legs down each side. We had to walk nearly to Fox House, but got going downhill, round Fox House had to get a man to stop me. We walked round to the road for Grindleford and got going again. We had another surprise when a horse in a field took fright and jumped over the wall. Down the hill we were in luck's way, a field gate was open in line with the road – we made for it and rolled off onto the grass. Arrived at Grindleford and had tea at my friend's great aunt. She sewed up my pants and we came home safe.

Now I was getting an expert rider, jumping from the step onto the saddle. But the 52 inch wheel was too large for me downhill. I rode to Wortley and had a good tea. Owlerton was a little village then, with stones to cross the river in Leppings Lane. The roads were not as good as they are today. At Wortley we stood before the camera, but nothing turned out. Coming home was nearly all downhill and my 52 inch wheel came in two.

Mounting the ordinary.

I went to a blacksmith's shop in Milton Street, and Chris Chappell and me pegged it, I blowed while he put some brass on it. I have been repairing from that time. I sold that mount at a profit and bought another one two inches smaller, a 50 inch wheel.

I was alright now, I could back pedal on this one and I could ride to Baslow without getting off. In those good old days many places gave us something to eat for nothing – 'we are pleased to have your company'. Baslow – tea, eggs and ham, bread and home-made jam, butter and cream all for ninepence. Eyam – Bull's Head facing church, long table with beef, ham, mutton, all kinds of sweets, cheese and pickles, cream in tea, go as you please, all for a shilling. Fox House – ginger ale, bread and cheese a penny-ha'penny. Farms and wild flowers, and we had the roads to ourselves. If we got behind a carrier's cart or a four-in-hand coach going uphill with the wind in front, we might get the long whip round our necks.

Outings and repairs on the ordinary

I was 18 years old now and sold the 50 inch wheel making twenty shillings profit. Bought another 50 inch wheel with taper roller bearings in the head and double row of roller bearings in the wheel hub. It had what were called cow-horn handlebars. I rode this for seven years, so I was riding what is called a penny-farthing for nine years in all. I think I did my fastest ride from Wortley nearly all downhill with wind behind, nearly seven miles, in 20 minutes, and broke three spokes. Now I became a cycle repairer. What a job it was to get the broken spokes out of the hub. I had to make tools, and drill with breastplate and rod with leather lace. On my new machine we went to Maltby, up Spital Hill and on Carlisle Street to miss the tramlines. We made a dingle with our bells and people came out to look at us. We had to ride on granite setts and round boulders, and the tramlines were worn with the dray and cart wheels. When going into Derbyshire we went round the back of the Midland station and Queen's Road. For Castleton and Ashopton we went to Malin Bridge, up towards Stannington and on the top side of Roscoe Wood and came out at the top of what is now Rivelin Road. I rode all the way to Maltby which was one of the finest villages in England, with red tiles, crags, Roche Abbey and Stone two miles on the road with a house built under the rock and a blacksmith's shop. We had tea here for fourpence. We saw a sham fight with redcoats, one soldier ran across a field in his red coat, looked over a wall, fired a shot and ran back, which made us laugh. Coming home it was getting dark and our lamps swinging in the middle of the wheel did not give much light. Going under the arch of the Midland Railway bridge at Tinsley I dropped in a hole which sent me over the front, and then when I got through the Great Central Railway arch I ran into a brick that sent me onto the footpath.

I rode to Rotherham when the Prince of Wales opened Clifton Park. It was a fine summer day, but coming home between Rotherham and Tinsley, the sky over Sheffield was as black as night, and after the storm passed over we were riding through water nearly twelve inches deep. In those days the roads all over Sheffield were round boulders, granite setts (flat square stones), and wood blocks which the rain lifted up. The horses soon made the roads slimy and slippery when wet.

I once had a drunken man betting me a quart he could throw me off – he rolled in front of me and over I came, but we had a knack of getting our feet on the ground first and it was a laugh. Another time a big fat policeman pushed his stick in my wheel and said he could not hear my bell, and that I could hurt a child. I think they would pinch us if they could. Some of the police were allowed to carry heavy sticks in those days.

Worksop and cricket

Whit-Monday. Up in the fields at daylight playing cricket, breakfast in the school at 7 o'clock. Then to Crookes recreation ground to sing Whitsuntide hymns – there were more than 100 over 18 years of age who walked from Cundy Street to sing. Then we went to the post office to send a telegram to the Golden Ball in Market Square at Worksop, for beds for six going on machines – our Cundy Street cricket club were to play Worksop on Whit-Tuesday. I was the youngest in the team, all our players wore white flannels with red and yellow striped jackets. We had a Yorkshire colt, a schoolmaster, our captain was Mr. Barnes – head of a steel foundry, and I was the boy. After we sent the telegram we had lunch and then on our machines and on our way. At Swallow Nest hill one of our riders, a six-footer on a 56 inch wheel fell off, sitting on the road with his legs between the spokes.

The inn was whitewashed and stood back then. The landlord and his wife slept out to make room for us. Ham and eggs for tea. In spite of what people say about the bad old days, we arrived full of life and were served like lords, the best of everything. After a good night's rest I was up at 6 o'clock for a 16 mile ride round Welbeck and through the tunnels, and back for breakfast – leg of mutton and ham to cut at with new-laid eggs and oatcakes all for one shilling and sixpence each. In the cricket match we won by an inning and a few runs. I bowled right through the match and took eight wickets, I was a fast bowler and weighed 11 stone. Afterwards we rode home. I liked cricket, but I liked my bicycle better. We did a lot of riding as far as Doncaster, Matlock, etc., every week. We were not a Sunday riding club, our rule was no riding on a Sunday, and when our Cundy Street club was playing Castleton they put me 12th man – the excuse was my riding there on the bicycle. I was in my 20th year now and weighed 12 stone – they called me little fatty on the football field.

To Boston

In 1886 six of our club members rode to Boston in a day. It was the last week in July and a hot summer day, over 90 degrees. We had breakfast at the Golden Ball in Market Square at Worksop for sixpence, and anything left on the table was wrapped up and put into our pockets. As I was getting on, one side of my handlebar came unscrewed, so I strapped an old file across with wire, and had one bar dropped and the other straight for over sixty miles. I cannot forget this ride, the roads were nothing like they are today, the country full of flowers, the beauty of the forest and the village of Budby. After Ollerton we stopped at a farmhouse where they were surprised that we had come from Sheffield and asked if we knew so-and-so in Sheffield. We had milk like cream and bread and cheese, as much as we could eat, and some for the pocket, all for nothing – they said they were pleased to have our company. Sweat, sweat and dust. When we got to Newark we had a shower bath before our dinner. Lady Harrington had just opened the hotel facing Newark castle. The ostler looked to our bicycles and to our surprise they were wiped down when we came out. But what a dinner – I think we had everything and we ate too much, all for tenpence. They could hardly believe we had ridden from Sheffield. We went through the market place for Sleaford Road, climbed the hill out of the town, and a grand sight we had with golden cornfields, sheep, pigs, cows, fowls and horses. Now we were on a road that was not a road – it was like a field each side, cornfields as far as we could see, and a lot of sheep grazing on the roadsides. The ruts in the road were over six inches deep and about twelve inches broad as the wheels on carts were very wide, and we had to ride in these ruts or where the horses walked. In those days a man would break stones to fill a hollow in the road, with dust and water, and then a big roller pulled by a horse.

We were getting tired with the hot sun and this bad road. At Leadenham, ten miles from Newark, we had a drink and a few pats on the back, about nine miles from Sleaford. Had tea at Sleaford for fourpence, but were getting tired now, what with the hot sun and dust, and seventeen miles to go. All flat roads and much better than from Newark. After seven miles we stopped for a drink, and Boston stump looked to be only a few miles away, but we were told it was five miles as the crow flies and ten by road. Arrived at 9-15 and were received with open arms at the oldest house in Boston, just over the bridge. There had been a crowd waiting for us, but gave up at 9 o'clock and went home. We were tired and the one with the bugle (the front rider had a horn to clear the road) was bad and had to go home in the train. We had a wash and supper and a good sleep in a big room, with thunderstorms. The first thing I did was to get my handlebar put right. I went to a blacksmith and I cleaned the thread and we tinned it with solder, cleaned the thread in the head, put solder in and made it warm and screwed the handlebar in. I had no more trouble with it.

We rode to Freiston Shore for the sports, and had boats for a shilling a day for four people. We had Yorkshire pudding, duck, fowl and roast beef. Everything was good. A captain from a trawler gave us a rock salmon about two feet long, this was a new fish. We said goodbye and thank you for a time we will not forget, and were on our way for Lincoln, where we were to stop for the night. After high tea we had a look round Lincoln and when we came back they had cleared the room for dancing, which went on until 3 o'clock. There was sloe wine, biscuits, and grapes, or home brewed beer with bread and cheese. One of our lads played a fiddle. One woman I danced with must have been about sixteen stone and called me a Sheffield waster as she kept putting her toes under my feet. All this with the tea, bed and breakfast for two shillings and sixpence. Our ride back was not of the highest class, when we were through East Markham one of our boys went over the handlebars and made his nose bleed, and then we tried a short-cut through the forest but the gamekeeper turned us back. But we arrived at the Golden Ball and they soon had a good tea for us. A week not to forget, all for seventeen shillings.

Herbert Smith with friends cycling to Boston in 1886.
The first rider's horn warns of their approach down the hill.

To Buxton

A ride to Buxton through three thunderstorms, sunshine, and strong winds. When I got through Ashford going round the bend for Taddington Dale I was blown from the saddle to sprawl on the road. Thunder and lightning going down the hill for Buxton in wet clothes. All I could do was to have something to eat and get on my way home. Coming down Taddington Dale there was a cloudburst with thunder and lightning – another shower-bath. Riding up Froggatt Edge I saw my front tyre was coming off half way round with the wet, so I had to do a bit of stringing up to get home – we always carried wire and string for such repairs. But I was in another thunderstorm when I left Fox House going uphill to Stony Ridge toll bar. The wind blew in my face and the rain was like buckets of water pouring over me into my shoes, and the road was a mess with white mud, but it was downhill to Hunter's Bar. Me and my bike were covered with this white mud and everybody was gazing at me, a boy was saying, "I bet he's been some way."

Things were changing very fast now, I had been riding the ordinary bicycle for nine years, and during that time I had been a dabbler in all sorts of things. I was sorry to part with it. I was still working at my trade hollow-ware buffing, and buffed 36 inch trays and silver cups 36 inches high. At the silver firm where I worked one of the finest ordinary bicycles was made with chased fancywork on the head and gilded – I was in that shop every minute I could.

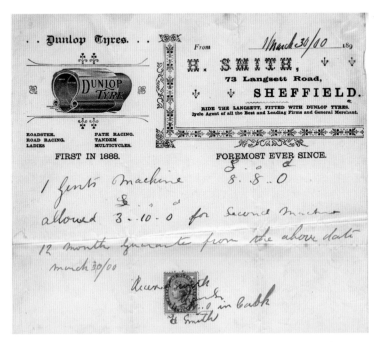

A bill dated 30th March 1900 for a gent's bicycle costing eight guineas, three pounds, ten shillings allowed for the exchanged bicycle.

I was secretary for the Neepsend Mission and we had our photograph taken at Neepsend station, it was like being in Sherwood Forest. I went for art lessons to Mr. Richard Turner in Alderson Road, Highfields. He was an artist at the college in Clarkehouse Road, I paid a shilling an hour. I had two candles, one at each side of the easel. He was a fine artist but I only went for six months for he was nearly always drunk.

Riding the safety

In 1884 when Dunlop made the tube for the bicycle tyre, all kinds of freaks were on the road. Tricycles with two large wheels and others with two small wheels and what were called the safety with a 28 or 30 inch front wheel and a 24 or 26 inch back wheel. We did not like giving up riding the big wheel for we could not forget the good times we had. There was many a dust-up about the safety bicycle – we would have it that if we had a full fall we had time to gather ourselves and save our fall, but with what they call the safety it was a three-quarter fall and you hit the road before you could say 'mun'! My first 'safety' had a straight tube from head to back forks, 28 inch front wheel, 26 inch back wheel, three-quarter inch tyres and a one inch block chain.

One of my first long rides on a safety bicycle was to Hull and back in a day in 1896. I left Sheffield about 6 o'clock a.m. and got to Booth for breakfast, ham and eggs for sixpence. At North Cave I called for a glass of milk and when I asked the farmer how much, he said nothing for he was pleased to have a little chat and "thars come allway from Sheffield this morning" and that I was to call on my way back. I had some friends about three miles down Holderness Road and by 1 o'clock I was sitting down with a plate of giblet pie in front of me. I called at the farm at North Cave on the way back, as promised, and the farmer smiled all over his face and said "come tha way in me lad, for tha welcome". He gave me two eggs and some cream and said that he did not want to be insulted when I wanted to pay. He wished me luck and a good day. When I returned to Booth Ferry for tea, it was ready for me – toasted tea cakes and home-made tarts and as many apples as I could carry. But she asked so many questions, nearly all about Sheffield Wednesday Football Club and one of the full-backs, I think she might have been in love with him!

I had another ride to Hull and called at Booth Ferry for breakfast again. The sun was shining and she wished me a good outing, and there was another happy smile at North Cave. In those days we could ride for miles and not see anything on the road, and these stops made it more enjoyable. When I arrived at Hull lunch was ready for me, and my friends had made arrangements for me to go to London on a trading ship. This was something new to me, we left Hull at 3 o'clock p.m. and arrived at London 3 o'clock p.m. the next day. These ships were not allowed passengers, so I had to keep out of sight while we got down the river, and the Port of London. The captain's wife was on the boat and I had my meals with them. My friend had made all the arrangements, and I had four hours in a bunk when one of the sailors came out on watch at twelve midnight. There was another passenger on board, he was an actor making for London. He did juggling tricks and he gave us a turn to pass the time. It was a grand calm ride and I got out of London Dock gates alright. I made my way to Houndsditch to look at toy shops, toys was one of my side-lines. I had lunch and then had to find the Great North Road. At last I was on the road to Peterborough. 11 o'clock was striking when I arrived, the porter was just closing the Station Hotel door, but he opened it for me and let me in. We were the Kings of the Road then and the landlords called us 'sir', and were pleased to have our company. I was soon in bed, and not having had much sleep the night on the boat, I did not need rocking. After breakfast I had a look round Peterborough, and then went on the North Road for Stamford. When I was near Grantham, I passed an inn and smelled a good smell. I went in and there was an open fire with a large stew-pot on chains. I was in time for dinner. Roast beef and Yorkshire pudding for ninepence with a cup of tea was a good foundation for my ride home, nearly sixty miles.

On another occasion I rode to Lincoln through the lanes and saw hundreds of sheep and only one man with his dog. The roads were very bad, but I found an inn with a fireplace large enough to sit under with the spit turning the meat. I got talking to the old grandfather, about eighty years old, smoking his long stem pipe. What a tale he could tell and how I enjoyed those tales. A lot were about the Lincolnshire coast smuggling and he pointed out farms where goods were carried to. I arrived at Spilsby where one of my friend's aunt lived. We went to the butcher for two pounds of rump steak and bought spuds and a loaf of bread and got it all ready ourselves. Afterwards I rode back to Lincoln, and home the next day.

I rode to Mablethorpe in 1896. I liked that run, everything was at its best. I have been every year since, for over forty-six years, and sixteen times there and back in the day. I started from home at 12 midnight. You see a lot of wildlife on the way, a fine fox at Gringley-on-the-Hill, rabbits on the road jumping and spinning round, and once I had a race after a hare, it ran for about two hundred yards and then all at once turned through the hedge. I will always remember these rides, seeing the sun rising.

A 1904 advertising calendar which Herbert Smith produced.

73 Langsett Road 1895-1905.
This was the shop which gave the name to the 'Langsett' bicycle.

The first cycle shops, 73 Langsett Road
and the first 'Langsett' bicycle.

I opened my first shop in 1890 in Springvale Road, and then in Wood Street. I was still working in the silver trade. Sheffield was not like some towns for bicycles, people said there were too many hills, but it was a new thing – it was a gold-rush, all kinds of people came in for bicycles.

The Drill Hall (Glossop Road) had a school to teach ladies to ride and it paid well. Roads were clear of traffic in those days and ladies had nothing to be afraid of. Some went to the Drill Hall and learned to ride unknown to their husbands before asking for a bicycle. I went with a lady for her to learn at what is now the police ground (Niagara Road). All this took a lot of our time up and we had to work late at night with poor gas light, oil lamps and candles.

But it was only a summer trade, the roads were bad and few people rode in winter, so I had to have side-lines – Captain Webb matches penny a dozen, elevenpence a gross box. Paraffin oil fivepence a gallon, penny-ha'penny a quart, penny a pint with a shuttlefeather given. Fireworks one shilling and threepence a gross, penny-ha'penny a dozen, Chinese crackers (72 on a string) a ha'penny, 84 large ones a penny. A one pint basin a penny, pint pots twopence each, pancheons from threepence ha'penny, peggy pots from one shilling and ninepence, wire netting from a penny per yard – ninepence per dozen yards. Toys from Germany – clockwork trains on lines fivepence-ha'penny. Quart tea can with swing handle and lid threepence-ha'penny.

In 1895 I moved into one of the shops which had been built on Langsett Road, number 73. It was the last shop away from the town which was a penny tramcar fare, and I could see sheep in the fields. Within twelve months I had competition from other shops selling cycles nearby. In 1896 I had to have a workshop as well as the shop because I had no room for the freaks of tricycles to repair, and I found one on Penistone Road.

Dunlop tyres

The first Dunlop tyre was a flat rim with yards of canvas wrapped round. Then the wired-on cover came out and you had to have a strong grip and knack to get one off and on without puncturing it with the levers. About 1899 I was one of many shopkeepers summonsed for fitting Dunlop tyre tubes inside covers which were not Dunlop. It cost me about £25. We had to go to London to fight the case but we were all served alike. All the covers were in court with labels on. Coming home it was snowing at Chesterfield and we could not see anything and did not hear the shout "change for Sheffield." And so we got to Leeds! It made it 6 o'clock a.m.

when we got home. In those days the compartments were small and no w.c., we had foot warmers when we left London but they were cold before we were half way home, and rugs around our legs, mufflers, gloves, and a good top coat. It seemed that all England was stripping tyres and fitting new Dunlops. I had solicitors' letters from Sheffield and London to say that they had pleaded for me. This trouble made some bankrupt. The talk was all about Dunlop tyres. A lot of ideas not to give up on the solid tyre and the cushion tyre, they were frightened of punctures. Although the covers were thick rubber, they still were punctured by scrap steel falling off drays. I saw the first bicycle with a new wired-on cover at the sports at Bramall Lane when it was a dirt-track – they put him a lap behind, but he won.

Cycle shows

I went to the first big show at Crystal Palace. I have been to shows at the Stanley show at Islington, Earl's Court, Olympia and Manchester every show but two which were due to illness. For Crystal Palace we left Sheffield at 12 midnight for two days, fare fourteen shillings. The little engine was half the size of the present day ones. About three and a half hours and a ten minute stop for a cup of tea if we got one. We had to tip the guard for foot warmers and then wrapped ourselves with rugs and heavy coats for the frosty and misty night. The train again the next day at 12 midnight. In those days everything we saw was something new. When we arrived the refreshment room was first, then to the underground for what we called the Puffing Billy – what smooth black walls. Book for the monument for Billingsgate market. I don't know what we looked like with our tall hats, but there were a lot more men wearing them, so it was fun. Strong men were running up the plank from the boats with boxes on their heads, no hands to guide but a heavy collar to keep the neck dry. Horses and drays and carts every way for a mile. Then for Smithfield, I saw as much meat there to last me a thousand years. Now to look for a place for bed and breakfast. We found one at the corner of Thames Embankment, it's been pulled down and I think it's a newspaper printing works now. We book at Blackfriars Bridge station, one shilling and sixpence return.

Crystal Palace was a place of light and everything was new to see. For one thing, we were counted with the nobs with our frock coats and top hats. There was the Dunlop team with their machines for four riders, it was a new thing to watch them trying to break a record going round the track. Four riders on one machine and then after two laps to get speed up, the rider on a single machine would slip behind, and another four men would be doing two laps to get up speed and the first four would glide off and the single rider slipped on the back of this one. This went on for one hour. They must have done that glide many times to be so perfect with it. The machine which had been ridden by the ten riders was inside the show.

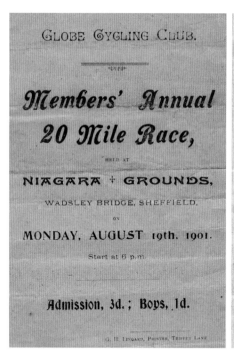

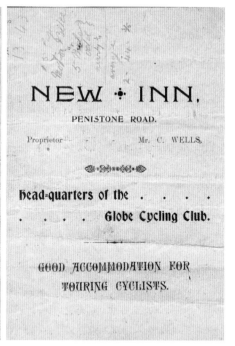

GLOBE CYCLING CLUB.

Members' Annual
20 Mile Race,

HELD AT

NIAGARA + GROUNDS,

WADSLEY BRIDGE, SHEFFIELD.

ON

MONDAY, AUGUST 19th. 1901.

Start at 6 p.m.

Admission, 3d.; Boys, 1d.

G. H. LINGARD, PRINTER, TRIPPET LANE.

OFFICIALS.

Judge—E. NEWTON.   Starter and Timekeeper—J. WALKER
Lap Superintendent—C. HARLOW.

PRIZES.

FIRST PRIZE.

Chappell's Cup - (to be won three times).
Also GOLD MEDAL (value Two Guineas),
Given by the Club.

SECOND PRIZE.

GOLD MEDAL - (value £1 15s.)
Given by the CLUB.

THIRD PRIZE.

SILVER MEDAL, Gold Centre,
Value 30s. given by the CLUB.

FOURTH PRIZE.

SPECIAL PRIZE,

Given by J. THOMPSON, Esq. (value 10/.

FIFTH PRIZE.

SPECIAL PRIZE,

Given by J. DENMAN, Esq., Retford, value 10/-.

COMPETITORS.

		Starts.
1—H. Watts (Sheffield)	...	Scratch.
2—J. Denman (Retford)	...	,,
3—W. Denman ,,	...	,,
4—W. Tootell ,,	...	,,
5—T. Abbott (Sheffield)	...	1 Minute.
6—P. Walker ,,	...	
7—W. Cressey ,,	...	2 Minutes.
8—G. H. Fearn ,,	...	4 Minutes.
9—J. Sutherland ,,	...	

RULES.

TWENTY MILES TRACK RACE.—Only members of the club shall be allowed to compete in this race, unless he be financial *four* weeks previous to the race. Pacing will be strictly prohibited. No competitor shall be allowed to single out and pace any one individual competitor; if he does so, and in the opinion of the judge it was an understanding between the two, the judge shall have power to disqualify both.

N.B.—The meaning of "pacing" in this rule is where one competitor waits upon another to pull him out away from the other competitors. The judges decision to be final.

That no member be allowed to compete in club races who has ridden at unlicensed or professional race meeting.

That every member to put in three runs before he is allowed to compete in any club race.

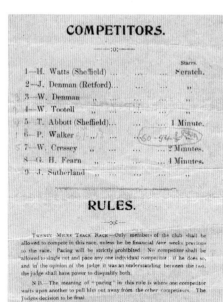

NEW + INN,

PENISTONE ROAD.

Proprietor   -   -   Mr. C. WELLS.

Head-quarters of the . . . .
. . . . Globe Cycling Club.

GOOD ACCOMMODATION FOR
TOURING CYCLISTS.

Herbert Smith's programme for the 1901 Globe Cycling Club annual race
at the Niagara track.

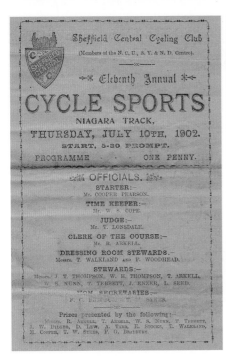
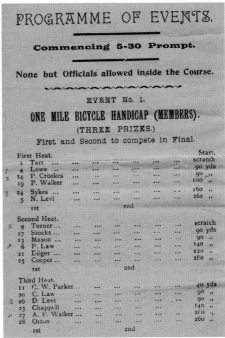
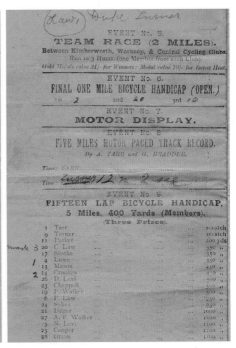

Herbert Smith's programme for the 1902 Sheffield Central C.C. Sports programme – his friends, C. Chappell and D. Levi are competitors.

Dunlop had a very large stand and a big office with drinks, tea or coffee with sandwiches and seats. What a display and how they could talk, these men were six feet and over and weigh sixteen to eighteen stone. Their frock coats and tall hats with gloves in were on the chairs on the stand, white shirt sleeves with cuffs turned up. They were telling us how easy it was to put on the rim without tyre levers, they did it and it looked easy. Every stand had advertisements and a fine office with plenty to eat and drink. I think some of the machines were got up for the eye, the ladies' with gold and the dress guard with silk fancy-work, and what prices! There were Pedersen machines (Dursley-Pedersen bicycles) weighing about 20 pounds, these were the lightest at the show, priced at 22 guineas. They tried to make us their Sheffield agent – I think they were looking at our top hats and not our pocket! There was not a machine in the show much under £20. Tricycles, tandems, machines for three and four riders. We got in the train with catalogues and lead pencils with names on and a good long day to remember.

The next day we took the things we did not want to carry to a cloakroom and went sightseeing. This is what I did at all the cycle shows. The Tower of London, Westminster Abbey, Bow Bells, St. Paul's, and I saw several shows at Drury Lane, and the first moving picture at Earl's Court – a prize fight from U.S.A., it was very poor, a lot of bright lights flickered in it.

Bicycle developments and the first Langsett

I might say that from 1894 to 1910 the fashion was for the tricycles and cycles which were first seen ridden by the Royal Family. Dukes, gents with tall hats and ladies with bustles. All skirts had to be held down with skirt clips. In 1894 some ladies and gents paid over £50 for tricycles and cycles, and by 1910 we could sell at eight guineas, but we could lose as much as five pounds if we had a cycle left over after the season. Dunlop were the covers to have but at a high price. Before 1910 I was fitting and sticking every kind of cover and rubber tyres. A lot of makers were trying to get over the Dunlop patent, one had a wire with a hook bent at each end which fitted in four holes in the rim, no rim brakes yet. The pneumatic brake had an oval rubber ball to squeeze, with a rubber pipe to a rubber ball with a thick face which expanded onto the tyre – these did not last long. When rim brakes came out they transferred the four wire ends to the centre of the rim between the spokes, and put a thread on the wire held by a small nut – Dunlop took this to court. There were covers laced up, others clipped through a hole at one side, then came the Fleury tyre with no inner tube, it was rubber with a broad tang, we put soft soap on and the air pressure held it down.

Up to 1900 bicycles and tricycle parts were not standard, we called them bastard parts, and had to tap the nuts to fit, make lugs and reduce hubs now free-wheels were coming out. I have a rim marker for 30, 28, 26 and 24 holes, I cut and tapped all the spokes which did not break – was good steel we worked with. About 1895 B.S.A. started selling what were called the B.S.A. standard fittings. I built the first B.S.A. lightweight bicycle in Sheffield and called it the Langsett Bicycle. I got the fittings from B.S.A. Cycle Co. Ltd. and the tubing from Crowleys which is now at Brightside. We called it trade tubing, it would twist but it would not break, and when brazed up rang like a bell. It was short wheelbase, 26 inch wheels, 21 pounds weight. People said it was too light, I had a lot of Sharrow gents down, standing on the bottom bracket to see if it twisted, and I built lightweights from that day.

All kinds of two-speed and three-speed gears were on the market, fighting against each other. Harry Green was riding about 1903 for the Fleet Cycle Co., I was their agent. He did a wonderful ride to John O'Groats with wind, rain and mud, advertising the Crabbe three-speed. This was on a light bicycle and his record stood for years. We cyclists were funny in our thoughts. They were gone on the Triumph that was sold on The Moor in Sheffield, which had nearly all the customers for new bicycles, and then I got the repairs. I had all the Sharrow Cyclists for repairs, and built machines for some of their members. I sold 'Stainless Stephen' (Mr. Bains) his first bicycle and had testimonials from Sharrow who had the records for Sheffield. Some of the jobs we got included a pair of Dunlop tyres to fit onto wheels for a trap, had to make strong tyre levers for prising them on, when he was driving away he said he was pleased with it. We had hansom cab wheels to stick rubbers on in the grooves, it was a nasty smelling job.

My landlord lived next door, and as I seemed to be doing well, he raised my rent by three pounds a year because I had put up a sign over the shop. I had a V-shaped window back with four large mirror glasses, one bicycle reflected in these with a few plants. With cycle sales reducing it was not wise to stock many. My workshop on Penistone Road was too far away, and so I took one in Whitehouse Lane where I could store goods and enamel the cycle frames. I had a good man who could turn his hand to anything. The tricycles for repair took up a lot of room and heating the cement for the solid tyres and cushion tyres was an unpleasant job. I had been advertising the B.S.A. bicycles built to your specification, and had a sign three feet long with the B.S.A. crossed guns trademark. Then I had a shock – B.S.A. made Mr. Wragg their sole agent and the sign had to come down. So I built my Langsett Bicycles with fittings supplied by the Cycle Components Mfg. Co., Birmingham. One customer worked in the silver plating shop at Walker & Hall, and he had all the parts on his bicycle silver plated. There was so much silver plate on, the spokes and everything had to be re-threaded. I enamelled it a chocolate colour with gold lines and new Langsett transfers. It cost over five pounds.

I bought a motor bicycle called the Fleet. This was about 1900 and it was the first mass-production machine in Sheffield and was an attraction for people to come and see. J. Haslam had been in my shop and I went with him to Leicester. We talked over making a motor cycle club, and when I got the motor bicycle I was the first member of the club which was called The Hallamshire Motor Cycle Club. I took it up Wadsley Bridge for Pitsmoor, it stopped all at once like a donkey sticking its front legs out. I had not been out with the club and I was tired of people taking up my time with it, so I sold it at a loss to Mr. Longbottom, the coal merchant. The Longbottoms were good people to work for.

Cycles for soldiers

After the Boer War I made friends with some of the soldiers at the nearby Hillsborough Barracks and this got me orders. In 1903 Major Butler gave me an order for twelve bicycles, so I got all the specifications, and two were for men over six feet tall and so had frames with double top tubes. This was the Monday and I had no parts in stock. I caught the first train to Birmingham at 4 o'clock the next morning, it was a slow train but I was there by 9 o'clock. I was lucky to get everything I needed for the twelve cycles including the two frames with double tubes. I brought the spokes and things I could carry back with me, and saw everything else packed on a dray for the railway station. I did not go to bed for two nights, I had the spokes to cut and tap, the rims to mark and drill with 40 holes rear and 32 front, the hubs to reduce and tap for the free-wheels to fit. I received all the goods by Wednesday morning and the twelve bicycles were in the barracks on Saturday morning. A letter from Major Butler came first post on Monday to say he was pleased with them, together with a cheque for over £100. I sold about fifty bicycles to the soldiers during the next three years, they had a photograph taken at the barracks. I was pally with the sergeants and would go into the barracks and the canteen any time. We went out on runs and we would have a revolver with six rounds. We could go for miles and not see anybody. One ride was to Haddon Hall, the soldiers went in free and I went in as an officer's servant. Another was to Welbeck Abbey and we called at the Golden Ball at Worksop, it had been rebuilt in front of the old house. The landlord had been a sergeant in the same company as my friends and we had a good lunch of roast beef etc. for no pay and a long stay. We had some good times both in the barracks and out in the country. It did me a lot of good in advertising my bicycles, for at that time I had competition from shops and house-shops within half a mile from me, and we had some wet summers. I had a trailer which I used and I put a sign on the back to advertise.

The soldiers at Hillsborough Barracks with their twelve Langsett bicycles in 1903. Four year old R.A. Smith is to the left of his father, with three other Langsett bicycle owners.

Time trials

In 1896, I joined the Yorkshire Road Club. We had to ride 100 miles in twelve hours. Two friends promised to pace me on a ride to Cleethorpes. We left Sheffield at 6 o'clock a.m. for Doncaster and Burringham Ferry, and had to cross the river in a boat. It was not a pleasant crossing as the tide was strong. Through Brigg and then Cleethorpes for dinner – cycling makes you eat well. I was asked to pace and we made the same way back, at the ferry we had to shout as loud as we could for the boat. The lanes look long and just room for a horse and cart, and rough at that. We got to Rotherham at half past eight, I left my two friends behind and made it home by 10 o'clock. Customers were waiting to hire bicycles for Sunday, and it was 12 midnight before I could close the shop. We did not open on Sundays and let the bicycles out on Saturday night, to be back by 9 o'clock on Monday morning, or pay for Monday. My two friends did not turn out when I did my next ride.

In 1897 I sent my subscription to the Yorkshire Road Club and then sent for record cards because I was going to try from Retford to York, about fifty-two miles. I rode to Retford and got checked. Fine day, wind alright and I felt well after my twenty-six miles ride to Retford. My two friends did not show up so I had to go on my own, and my first time on that part of the Great North Road. I was riding well. When I got to Scrooby I could see Chris Chappell with a tandem pair in front pacing him along, he got the record that day. While I was watching this and thinking of my best plan my eyes were off the road, and when I looked I saw a shoe sole in front. I just missed it with the front wheel, but my back got it and that did it. It took a long time to repair the punctures and there was no-one to shout at over my bad luck, only the little birds which tried to cheer me up with their songs. After the repairs I rode to Doncaster for lunch, but when I got going downhill at Hooton Roberts my chain caught on the crank and pulled my cycle out of track. After that I made chain guards.

I was still working in the silver trade and when I got home I was cycle repairing or picture framing, so did not have much time for my training runs. But I wrote to The Yorkshire Road Club for another card. This time I went to York. I was working in Tudor Street, buffing, until 1 o'clock, and had to catch the train from Victoria Station at quarter past. I just got it (it got me as well – I was all of a sweat!). I had lunch on the train and at York had to find the starting place which was the Post Office, to be checked. I was riding my own B.S.A. fittings bicycle, short wheelbase, 26 inch wheels steel rims, 84 inch gear and no brakes. We did not require brakes as there was no traffic on the road. My so-called pals did not turn up and I was left on my own again. They were to pace me, get the railway gate open and give me a drink which I did not get. Also I had to find my way, following the telegraph wires was a good idea. At Deighton Grove about eight miles from York, a lad on a tricycle came out of a side road with his front wheel in front of me. I went over the bars in a flash and was in the road much shaken. The lad was alright but his front rim was broken and his rubber tyre. My watch glass was broken, and my cycle meter, but nothing else. When I arrived at Selby, Chris Chappell was there helping someone riding to Bridlington. He signed his name and the time and said, "my word, Smith, you're riding well." I did not say that I had had a fall. There were no wicket gates at the railway crossings and I had no help and no brakes with an 84 inch gear to pull up. An old man or woman would unlock the gates each time. At Doncaster I was delayed getting my card signed at a cycle shop because the man was in his workshop at the end of his long garden. When I was about a hundred yards before the railway crossing at Sutton the gate was closed and that lost me over five minutes. A gold medal was for a time under three hours from York to Retford. My time was three hours and five minutes, which was the silver medal, so the lad on the tricycle, Sutton Crossing, and my friends not turning up lost me the gold medal. I was twenty-five minutes off the record, Chris Chappell was the record man, two hours forty minutes. He was paced to Doncaster and then to Selby and then to York. After all my bad luck I did not try again in a time trial.

In club life I was secretary with Cundy Street for six years until 1890, then Neepsend, and joined Sheffield Central in 1894. I had no time for racing, but I did some pacing with Chris Chappell. Mr. Lister had his collar bone broken on Bramley Hill, he was run into from a side lane as the club was going to Tickhill. Mrs. Lister rode from London to Sheffield. We went to Newark. In those days not all riders were honest when pacing, some tricks were – to be pulled by strong elastic when no one in sight (the elastic in the pacer's pocket), to get a ride in a cab or to catch a train for a few miles. For a record ride you only had to write to the club secretary and pay your entrance fee to get your card. You had it signed with the time you commenced your ride, any person could sign with the time of day. The Sheffield Central Cycling Club was only a Thursday club then (Sheffield early closing day), we were nearly all shopkeepers or employed in shops. We went on the Great North Road from Doncaster at what we called the Red House to Sutton Crossing and back for twenty-five miles. Fifty miles was from Babworth Lane through Doncaster by the race course to Thorne and back.

A home for the family, 64 Langsett Road and track racing

(In 1904 the family made their home away from the Langsett Road cycle shop. They went to Wadsley village and then lived at a second shop which Herbert's wife, Sarah, looked after for extra income. After moving several times they returned to live above the shop at 64 Langsett Road.)

In 1898, 22nd June, I was married and went to Mablethorpe for fourteen days for our honeymoon. Mablethorpe was not known then, it was only one street with a few shops. Our first child, Rupert Allan, was born 22nd May 1899, and our second, Edward Stuart 22nd February 1901. Our third, Eveline was born 30th November 1903. All were born at 73 Langsett Road. Our dog, Grip, was very protective with the children. When my oldest was about five years of age we went to live in the village of Wadsley, in those days it was all fields from Hillsborough, but it was not pleasant me going home late at night, 12 o'clock on Saturdays, for people had been stopped and hurt and robbed. I went home on my bicycle sometimes up Far Lane and sometimes up Wadsley Lane. We had 40 fowls, 2 geese, 2 pigs, a large croft and a garden with a William pear tree. A farm was across the lane. We did not stay long. We went to Blackpool for a day trip and when we came back and lit the lamp – there was no gas for we were out of Sheffield – and the walls were covered with black-clocks. When we went to Wadsley it was late spring and the family had hooping-cough (whooping-cough, old spelling) but it cured them, the air on Wadsley Common cannot be found anywhere better. We had to go to Lodge Moor Hospital for all three children, the oldest boy and the girl with scarlet fever, the youngest boy with diphtheria. We advertised the cottage and fowls etc. and soon sold. We took another shop up Chesterfield Road just above Meersbrook Park Road with a tram stop there, but we had not been there long when the cars went higher up the road to Woodbank Crescent and that spoilt our stand. These shops were new and there were a lot of crickets making their noise and flying about. We thought we would do better if we went to Heeley Bottom. We had to leave here as it was not a paying shop and very dirty. It took my time up riding there and back over the tram setts, my man did

Edward Smith age five in 1906 on his tricycle horse. It was while riding this at the bottom of Derbyshire Lane, off Chesterfield Road, that he fell down the open hatch of a public house when the beer was being delivered and suffered a broken nose.

not take his wage some weeks. The winter was wet with some snow. My second boy had diphtheria here, he had been riding his tricycle horse. He was a good skater for his age. I made two small cycles and the two boys were soon riding and we all went out together, I had my trailer with the young girl in it.

There were some new shops built on Middlewood Road, at the bottom of Crofton Avenue at Hillsborough and we flitted there. It was here that our girl was ill with scarlet fever. Hillsborough and Heeley were only like villages then and there was no traffic on the roads, only milk carts, I was a few years too soon in opening these shops. With having these shops at Heeley that year I rode 16,000 miles. I was riding 14,000 miles nearly every year going out with the club and with customers.

The Middlewood Road shop was so damp, there was a spring running underneath and when it rained everything was wet, so we were glad to get out. It was alright for the children on their cycles and the girl in the trailer – no traffic on the road. At the bottom of Crofton Avenue water from the River Don ran into Middlewood Road and a deep drop, it has all been filled up now. There was a house in Minto Road and we went there, but not for long, for there was a shop to let where the Co-op is now, and we went there. We had a go for another shop where we could make a good home but we had no luck.

64 Langsett Road, 1905

In 1905 there was a shop empty at 64 Langsett Road, opposite, which was the better side of the road. This was £18 a year, but I had to pay £23 because the person next door spoke about having it. I had a plate glass window put in and then had the middle wall taken down. I had some home-made motor bicycles with twin-cylinder engines, chain driven. These were too heavy and took up too much room so I let them go. We had mantles on the gas burners now and a lot more light, one was 600 candle power and hissed like a steam engine. It had a 30 inch chimney about five inches across, and when lit you could feel the heat all over the shop. About 1906 the motor and motor bicycle had come to stay and were sold on easy payments. The bicycle was starting to have a poor name, such as the old bedstead, etc. Frames were coming from foreign countries. The slump had come, bicycles with a three-speed fitted were priced as low as £3-19-6, and foreign bicycles cost about £2.

Track racing, Scarborough and the Isle of Wight, 1906

My first race on the Niagara Ground was in 1906 with the Sheffield Central. Seventy-two laps, twenty-five miles. Thirty-six riders on the track, one with the Sheffield record. My start was three minutes. I rode to see what it was like going round with a lot of good and fast men hanging on to one another's back wheels. I entered in 1907 and this time they gave me seven minutes, there were thirty riders, the long mark man had twenty-five minutes start. Some had ten or twelve and fifteen or twenty minutes start with three laps in hand. I finally got my name on the Enfield cup on 19th August 1909.

Herbert Smith in 1909 after winning the
Sheffield Central Cycling Club Enfield Cup.

In September, 1906 I went with my brother-in-law for a two day ride to one of my travellers who had an hotel in Scarborough. We left home at 6 o'clock a.m. My friend rode half a wheel in front of me, I let him do it for there was no wind, and when we got to Selby he was done and we had to stop for a time, but after a good dinner at York he came round. It was 90 degrees in the shade and at New Malton it was 95 degrees. Next day we came back over Foxholes to Driffield and it was still over 90 degrees, and September at that – we did sweat. One customer was from Birley Carr, we went to London and then to Portsmouth. At Guildford we stopped at a posh hotel, and had rump steak, baked spuds etc. and were charged two shillings and sixpence. My friend did not like it, he thought it was too much. When we crossed for the Isle of Wight we had a shilling more than our ticket to pay for the bicycle. We went round the island and on coming home called at Windsor and on through Beaconsfield, we stopped here for the night with the town crier and he had some good stories to tell us. We went to the hotel for breakfast and then for Derby and home.

One February I went to the Manchester Cycle Show. Coming home the weather changed, it snowed with frozen ruts in the road and I got home very cold and hungry. Another time I went to Manchester on a tandem. We were going down Deansgate when a cycle rider came out of a side street and rode right into the middle of our machine. We came off and I rolled in front of the tram horses and hurt my kneecap.

Before the First World War we had a lot of pot-holes. All motors had solid tyres and the road was not made for them, it made it bad for the cycle rider bumping in these. On the Sunday before the Doncaster Races you would see all kinds of people on the road heading there. This is when I was going for a few days holiday, I nearly always went on the Sunday before the races. At Doncaster I remember a Punch and Judy show, six men sitting round a fire with a big tin on it, a lot of gypsies with caravans, man and wife with youngsters and donkeys, traps and carriages. It was nothing to go on the course and you always had something to see, many a time the King or the Prince of Wales.

Difficult times and the First World War

A railway strike. The wife and youngsters at the seaside and there were no motors to get them home then. There was nothing doing while the strike was on. One of my customers who had a shop himself explained how things went with him – he told me that one year it seemed that money rolled into his shop door, and then it started rolling out and he could not stop it. We had another collier coal strike and it was a bad time and a wet summer, we could have closed the shop all week for we were doing nothing. And then we came back on the shop (to live above the shop at 64 Langsett Road). To pull myself round I went to see a friend with some workshops with steam power, then I bought a buffing spindle and went to Huttons and Walker & Halls to see people I worked for 10 years before and I soon got going again, but it was heavy work, 24 inch trays and dish covers. I did this hollow-ware buffing for about twelve months and then the 1914 war broke out. During that war there were no easy payments and you had to pay cash. In 1914 I was in my forty-eighth year, but I had two good men who could make anything and a good wife. With these and myself to look after and many hours looking after the shop I did not get much bed. Many of my old customers came rolling in and brought new ones. Nearly everyone was going on making shells, I went and did a bit of turning but I had too much to do to follow it up. The cycles were selling now and the price was going up so we started to make any cycle which was on a good frame. Being the oldest cycle trader in Sheffield helped me a lot.

The Government was asking for suggestions to be sent in to bring the Zeppelins down. I sent one in and had a reply by return telling me it was going to the round table. About three weeks after, close it down with thank you. It was strange that the Zeppelin which was brought down at Mablethorpe was with the same idea I had sent up. This was a rocket to burst with live arrows, the arrows to be hollow to hold fire. I was told at Mablethorpe it was a thing which was burning stuck in the side that set the Zeppelin on fire. There was a show at the Cutlers' Hall showing these things and the advertisement mentioned the arrow, and when I went to look there was the place to hold it, but no arrow. We saw the Zeppelin go over the barracks and over Parkwood Springs, and we went on the Bole Hills three times when they were dropping bombs. It was a pull up Burgoyne Road, Cundy Street and Fir Street. There were hundreds of people up there, we could see the flashes and hear the bombs.

During this time I saw a lot of damage. I was going to London every three weeks. I was doing all kinds of side-lines and that meant me going to Birmingham, Liverpool and Manchester, and I got a good supply of cycle goods by going about. But it meant day and night work. I left home at 7 o'clock to Manchester for Brown Brothers and Runwell, down Deansgate and I was back at 4 o'clock with some special goods I wanted. It was all cash, but I got ¾%, and sometimes 5%, discount. I got the Journal for toys, cycles and hardware and I went for anything we could sell. I took my oldest son to London one time, we bought all one firm had in electric torches, and we saw some of the damage they had done, like Sheffield, we thought it was a lot then. I could not have done half of what I did without my wife which was something to be thankful for, and my children had a good mother.

We had to work under bad light, poor gas light with no light in the windows and blackout in the streets. With having the Toy Journal I found an address and got luminous paint and buttons, we painted the buttons and my son sat on a chair holding them to the bit of light we had to make them shine in the dark. We had queues for them and we must have sold thousands from a ha'penny to sixpence each. While in London and on Snow Hill in Birmingham I got a lot of pipe lighters and parts such as springs, wicks and wheels. How they sold. I got in with a new firm at Liverpool making sleeping dolls and we sold them faster than we could get them. These people were trying to get the German trade. I had been getting toys and mantles from Germany and many firms were trying to make these. In the last year of the war, toys were coming from Japan. I bought a large case from Whitecross Street (London), there was fifteen pounds' worth in it. Rocking horses and small horses and carts packed between the legs.

In August 1918 I left home at 6 o'clock in the morning and cycled to Newark for breakfast with my wife's cousin, and so I then had a mate on the road. About 1 o'clock we had a good dinner with Yorkshire pudding, it was lucky to get such meals without coupons, and they would be fined if they were caught. When I got to Biggleswade at about 6 o'clock I signed my name in the book. N. Green was in it, and Mills, and all the old record cyclists' names too. One hundred and forty miles, stop here for the night, up early. Rode to High Barnet, left my cycle at the station cloakroom and caught a bus for London. I made my way to Houndsditch, first thing to the baths and a good wash down, then for Whitecross Street. Here I bought thirty gross of snake torches made in Japan. I had been buying them in Sheffield when I could get them, I got the last two cases and three shillings a gross cheaper. Chater-Lea were only a few minutes away, I gave them a call and then had lunch. Then a bus for High Barnet and collected my cycle. The sun was shining and I was looking forward to a grand time. But before I reached Hatfield, what a storm. It thundered with lightning flashing all around. And the rain – I should say it was a water spout, the road was a river and I was wet to the skin, my cape was no good. I had made my plan to stay the night at Biggleswade but when I arrived I was too wet to stop. They gave me a good tea and then I went to Sandy and caught the 6 o'clock train, a slow train and I arrived at Grantham at 8 o'clock. The next train was due at Retford just after twelve. I was still wet and it was a fine evening so I got on the bicycle to ride the thirty miles. When near Newark there were soldiers having a night march and they were over the crown of the road. At the Market Place a baker put me on the right road, it was a dark night but the road was a whitish ribbon. I was lucky to have the wind at the back and one good thing, there were no motors on the road. At Markham Moor my back and front lights went out. I could hear my cycle meter clicking and it sounded like a big noise to me. I was in luck's way at Retford, it was so dark I was lost, but a man came out of a side street, he was an engine driver coming to work and he took me to the station. Got my ticket and in ten minutes was in the train for Sheffield. Arrived home, a good rub down and a little sleep, and in shop for 9 o'clock. There was a queue for the snake torches, twopence each. The shop was open every day from half past eight until 10 or 11 o'clock p.m., 1 o'clock Thursday afternoons. Sometimes on Saturdays we would be selling records until midnight and we had such poor lights we could not see what they were picking up. Once we had about twelve soldiers who had been drinking and when they had gone so had a box of two and sixpenny records, two dozen all alike.

We had no cycle club now, we had closed down and put ten pounds in the War Loan, for we had no time for club riding. Every person up to fifty years of age was called up to do something. I was fifty-one years old and I had to take my birth certificate to the drill hall. My oldest boy was a draughtsman in a drawing office and had been exempt as they could not spare him from his work, but he had his calling-up papers when he was nineteen. He was at Mablethorpe with his mother when I received these and I had to go and tell him. I left Sheffield at 12 midnight after a hard day's work, I wanted a little sleep but I did not get it. At fifty-one years of age it was a long ride to Mablethorpe and back in a day, and a hot summer day, as well as the way we were working during the war. So we left Mablethorpe to catch the 6 o'clock train from Gainsborough, but when we arrived that Sunday the train was not running. There was nothing for it but to ride home. When we were two miles through Bawtry I fell asleep while riding, it was a grand evening so I lay down and slept. My son woke me up, but I had to rest three more times after that. When we were at Tinsley I told my son to get home. I was three hours coming from Bawtry and that was the last time I rode to Mablethorpe and back in a day.

My next long ride was to Tunbridge Wells, my son was in the army camp there. My first stop was for the night at Leighton Buzzard. I had to sleep on a couch, every place was so full and food was short, but I was up early and got new laid eggs and had some bacon with them which was a good foundation. I had a snack in London and at Tonbridge I called at an inn and had the first cut of the beef with Yorkshire pudding for a shilling with no coupons. Oh, I did enjoy it. My son had a pass for a night out and we went to this inn for a good dinner. Coming home I made my way to Chatham and crossed the river at Gravesend. I had a dinner at a workmen's canteen without coupons again. It was a very hot day and I called at an old inn at Bishop's Stortford for a drink – which wasps enjoyed as well! Then to Royston where there was a German prison camp, and the prisoners were working on the farms, and plenty of land girls. No-one had any drinks and not a bed to sleep on, I was advised to go to the next village about ten miles down the road. I went that way. It was a fine warm night and it was like daylight. A corn stack made my bed that night, I made the best of it and got up early, cycled to Huntingdon and was there for 8 o'clock. All I had for breakfast was a roll, a bit of butter and a small pot of tea, so I had to get another egg out of my bag. At Stamford I had a dinner at the railway station. But while I had been sleeping on the corn stack, two German prisoners escaped – if they had found me I should have had good company. I was well away when I left Stamford, I had a few places I knew for drinks and a tea and home. Another good outing with no bad news from home, no rain and all sunshine.

The end of the War

In the last year of the War the shop was full every night with lads and their girls buying records, and enquiring about new machines. We were building a lightweight 'Langsett' again now and we had a house off the shop at the top of Bowness Road. I had trouble with the Income Tax inspector, but it was nothing like it is today. They worked on three years, but it went up from one shilling in the pound to five shillings in the pound. With the three year plan, I understood that if you had a big loss in one of the three years, you were allowed it. We were allowed, I think, five pounds a week earned income. The last year of the War I had an Income Tax sent me for £89 and I had to go many times to a small office in Fargate to state my case, and they put all sorts of questions to catch me before they made it much smaller. Our Langsett Lightweights were £16 to £20 now, for the building up was on the slow side and I had to go to London for the Chater-Lea fittings, and to Birmingham for the fittings from the Components Company. We were not doing B.S.A. fittings as I have said. The First World War was nothing like the Second World War. The workmen and the women workers were doing well and spending well. I went to Manchester and ordered a lot of flags and I went to Birmingham and ordered some more flags for we were looking for the War to be over soon. I joined a friend in sending a cheque to Dunlop for £150 for covers and tubes. We received half and it was nearly six months before we got the next lot, but the best of it is, in the meantime when I sent my order for some more, they wrote to me for a trade reference, when they still had over £70 in hand for so long. I wrote by return – you have had £70 in hand for so long and you ask for a trade reference, how many do you want and I will oblige you. I had a good reply by return and the tyres and tubes three days after, and we have been pals from that time. I was doing a lot of riding, getting goods of all kinds and we were expecting five crates of rocking horses, advertised in the Toy Journal. They were made in a forest in Ireland and they had a bank draft for £150. I was advised they were on their way, and what a grand sight when they arrived. They went all over Sheffield and some outside and the next lot were nearly all sold before I got them. I lost a small discount as Mr. May was made their Sheffield agent. It was risky sending a bank draft to Ireland, but it came off. My eldest son was in luck's way, the regiment was sent to Germany. He was transferred to Signal Corps and sent to Newcastle and not to France and so he got a few days at home. We were having bull weeks every week now and if we did not look for goods no-one would look for you, there were no travellers calling and that was it. My wife was a big help to our business and our boy and girl worked, just now it was records and cycles, also repairing gramophones with new springs and repairing speakers. When the War was over on 11th November 1918, my wife and son and daughter with several others helping, were selling flags and fireworks. Outside the shop there was an inspector and two policemen keeping the queue in order, they were coming in the shop door and going out at the back. It was my birthday, I was 52 years old, so what a birthday. I had saved so many fireworks there were bangs until midnight. After this news we could have more light and more window display to make things look more cheerful, but I still had to do a lot of cycling to get things in for there was a good supply of money yet and plenty of orders on the firm's books, but these orders had to be made to prices quoted when ordered. Overtime was stopped as there was no shell making. A lot of women were out of work and the people who spent the money wanted higher wages which would make the firms lose money, and men were stopping work and coming out on strike. This was going on up to 1926. There were the unemployed almost in rags marching to the town hall and there were nearly riots, but there were a lot of people who had saved money and were buying high-class cycles. Gilbert made a big improvement in the tone of the gramophone and there was a boom on it. After that the cat's whisker talking machine came out and I was lucky with both of these. I was one of Gilbert's first customers when he was going round with rubber heels (cheap shoes) in 1900, and he helped me all he could. He gave instructions that I was to have what I wanted, and gave me first chance for the Burndept gramophone for half price, Burndept had made so many patents and lost money. Needham's manager let me have the earphones and cat's whiskers that I wanted, and would tell me when a consignment was coming in.

Sheffield Central Cycling Club

The roads were not so good with a lot of potholes. I was getting out for a run on Thursdays, I had been to Matlock Bath and on coming back I met Mr. D. Levi near the Peacock Inn. He told me that he had been trying to get the Sheffield Central Cycle Club going again, but he said that he had no luck and asked me if I would try and I promised I would. When I did get the Club going again, there were many wanting to join who were out of work, so I took their subscriptions by small payments. For the first meeting I called I had a room at The Angel in Snig Hill and over thirty attended it, and we got going. One thing was the ten pounds club money in the War Loan. We had a lot of trouble getting it – we had not signed for it and the bank would not pay it. I got Mr. Oldham to go in again, he had been a member before the War and he was the manager of Raleigh Cycle Co. He knew the bank manager and that was how we got the ten pounds handed over.

It was not long before we had fifty new members, but we had more members out of work than in work. We were only a Thursday club for about six months, I think it was about 1920 when we had our first 25 miles race from Red House at Doncaster to Sutton Crossing and back. I rode to encourage the young members. At the next general meeting we had just received the ten pounds, and I moved that we bought a silver cup with this money and called it The Sheffield Central Cycling Club Memorial Race Cup. All the members out of work voted against it. Then I went in for a dance and went to the baths (Glossop Road baths) and had a chat with the manager. I moved that all members have tickets at one shilling each. I lost the vote again, but on that dance we made £14 profit and I had the price reduced for members and you'd be surprised what good it did. Then I got New Year's Eve and we made £40. During the time I was treasurer we had in the bank at one time just over £100, and at a dinner we had over one hundred and fifty sat down. I got the ten pounds for the Memorial Cup, and I got a social secretary, and then a racing secretary. We had a good dinner at Cockayne's in Snig Hill. Mr. Coburn, Palmer's traveller, was a star turn with funny yarns, and he got Palmer Tyre Company to give us a cup. And we got another cup from Palmer's, Rotherham wheelers got it, this was for the best all-rounder.

We made the Club a Thursday, Saturday and Sunday club. The first Sunday was to Miller's Dale, we had over fifty members there. Now we had a new cup for a Saturday race, an Open Memorial Race, and a Thursday race. We had garden parties every year with strawberries, we had over a hundred for tea at Edale, and we had football matches and surprise runs. My oldest son was Sunday Captain. For one surprise run I asked one of our members who was a butcher for a nice joint of meat and we got it to Mrs. Marriott at Eyam and she cooked it with spuds, greens and Yorkshire pudding, bread and a cup of tea. There were forty-five to sit down, this was the surprise run, with much talk after it. I forget what it cost me. After dinner we went into a field and played football. Just after we were nicely away the farmer came with a policeman, but we had gone. There was a big change with runs in these new club days from the old club days before the War when we were the Sheffield Central Thursday Cycling Club. We used to have some good places to go to for high teas, often with ham and eggs for ninepence, a shilling or one shilling and threepence. At one place at Retford we had chicken and ham, stewed fruits and sweets for one shilling and sixpence. Look at the changeover, I went on nearly all the club runs on Thursday and Sunday and had tea, on one run to Edwinstowe we had a hundred members out and what a fight it was for a cup of tea, and a charge of sixpence for it, and many times the pots were filled with warm water. Another time at the Taddington Dale Hotel the landlady was asking a shilling each for tea only, after a little bit of talking I gave her a note and asked if that would do. When we were near Buxton we stopped and counted up and it was sixpence each and not a shilling as the lady wanted.

We had to make a rule that all new members be recommended by a member and passed by the committee. This was keeping the Club clean. The Club was called the snobs, but we did not mind that. All our dancing programmes paid. Fancy dress – one of our old geared-up ordinary bicycles was lent to a member and he won first prize, another time he rode it to Monyash. We had the Enfield Cup for Thursday, new Cup for Saturday and the Memorial for open events. Palmer Cup, Nunn Cup and Levi Cup and then the gold medals which we cannot get today. We had a good display at our dinners when many of our members' mothers and fathers were there, and we had to refuse many tickets. At the general meetings we could not do anything right for a few members, which was not good for the Club. They sold no tickets for the dances, the Club was even called 'The Smith Club', for nearly every run had Smiths, sometimes four out with the Club. My youngest son, Edward, won nearly every race he rode in, he had second for Sheffield for 25 to 100 miles for over three years, and we had books with records of all racing etc. that the Club was doing. We had advertising from cycling firms which helped to pay for these and we saved money by holding our committee meetings at Mr. D. Levi's shop. The Club took a lot of my and my older son, Allan's, time to try to make it a success. We rode in all the 25 miles, and Allan won the Telegraph Cup. At one of our twelve hours we fixed a table at the front of the chapel on the green, but some of our members objected to it, so we had to move it across the road towards Finningley.

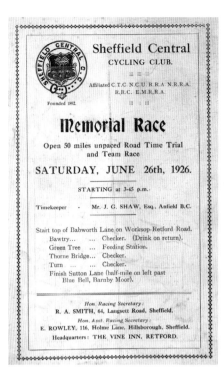

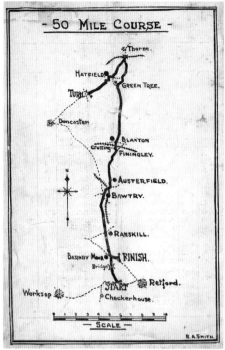

Sheffield Central CYCLING CLUB.

Affiliated C.T.C. N.C.U. R.R.A. N.R.R.A. R.R.C. E.M.R.R.A.

Founded 1892.

Memorial Race

Open 50 miles unpaced Road Time Trial and Team Race

SATURDAY, JUNE 26th, 1926.

STARTING at 3-45 p.m.

Timekeeper - Mr. J. G. SHAW, Esq., Anfield B.C.

Start top of Babworth Lane on Worksop-Retford Road.
Bawtry... ... Checker. (Drink on return).
Green Tree. ... Feeding Station.
Thorne Bridge... Checker.
Turn ... ... Checker.
Finish Sutton Lane (half-mile on left past Blue Bell, Barnby Moor).

Hon. Racing Secretary:
R. A. SMITH, 64, Langsett Road, Sheffield.
Hon. Asst. Racing Secretary:
E. ROWLEY, 116, Holme Lane, Hillsborough, Sheffield.
Headquarters: THE VINE INN, RETFORD.

- 50 MILE COURSE -

No.	Time of Start	Name	Club	Handicap Minute	No.	Time of Start	Name	Club	Handicap Minutes
1	3 45	W. Tinkler ...	Notts Castle	11	28	4 12	C. H. Salt ...	Clowne Wheelers	1
2	3 46	E. Dolby ...	Clowne Wheelers	10	29	4 13	W. T. Watkinson	Darnall 3 in H.	11
3	3 47	J. Hardy ...	Gainsboro' Wheelers	7	30	4 14	P. J. Emerson	Gainsboro' Wheelers	18
4	3 48	F. Austin ...	Sheffield Century	11	31	4 15	H. M. Finlay	Sheffield Central	9
5	3 49	G. O. Stanley	Mansfield Vict.	8	32	4 16	L. Ingle ...	Rutland C.C.	12
6	3 50	E. W. Eadon	Sheffield Central	20	33	4 17	W. Ball ...	Rotherham Wheelers	9
7	3 51	J. Salt ...	Clowne Wheelers	7	34	4 18	C. T. Lawrence	Notts Castle	2
8	3 52	W. A. Haslam	Sheffield Unity	13	35	4 19	J. Clayton ...	Sheffield Central	12
9	3 53	F. Mottram...	Sheffield Central	16	36	4 20	F. H. Harlow	Sheffield Century	10
10	3 54	H. Dawes ...	Mansfield Vict.	5	37	4 21	C. Marshall...	Gainsboro' Wheelers	11
11	3 55	W. Sharp ...	Notts Castle	10	38	4 22	S. J. Allison...	Notts Castle	6
12	3 56	G. B. Gamble	Leicester R.C.	12	39	4 23	W. B. Yarnold	Sharrow C.C.	11
13	3 57	G. E. Skaith	Gainsboro' Wheelers	2	40	4 24	F. Wagstaff...	Sheffield Central	5
14	3 58	G. Crookes ...	Mansfield Vict.	6	41	4 25	W. Wright ...	Sheffield Century	16
15	3 59	J. W. Berrisford	Notts Castle	13	42	4 26	E. Allen ...	Notts Castle	6
16	4 0	W. G. Griffin	Rotherham Wheelers	11	43	4 27	C. E. Bingley	Endcliffe C.C.	13
17	4 1	J. Willers ...	Sheffield Central	13	44	4 28	A. Nortrop ...	Rotherham Wheelers	9
18	4 2	F. Bennett ...	Darnall 3 in H.	6	45	4 29	E. S. Smith...	Sheffield Central	7
19	4 3	E. Thackeray	Sheffield Central	14	46	4 30	C. Saxton ...	Mansfield Vict.	11
20	4 4	P. J. Jarvis ...	Notts Castle	7	47	4 31	A. E. Page ...	Sheffield Century	15
21	4 5	W. H. Trenchard	Sheffield Central	10	48	4 32	J. C. Bingham	Sheffield Sports	12
22	4 6	T. Wells ...	Mansfield Vict.	9	49	4 33	C. E. Snowden	Notts Castle	Scr.
23	4 7	G. M. Bennett	Sharrow C.C.	10	50	4 34	T. Wagstaff...	Sheffield Central	8
24	4 8	H. A. Wilkie ...	Sheffield Century	7	51	4 35	A. Huckle ...	Rotherham Wheelers	11
25	4 9	J. Greaves ...	Clowne Wheelers	10	52	4 36	R. H. Lawrence	Notts Castle	9
26	4 10	F. A. Adams ...	Sheffield Sports	15	53	4 37	F. Nugent ...	Sheffield Central	8
27	4 11	W. Lawrence	Notts Castle	10	54	4 38	J. B. Salt ...	Clowne Wheelers	4

Sheffield Central C.C. 1926 50 miles time trial with map of the course drawn by R.A. Smith. E.S. Smith is number 45.

When I resigned in 1926 I was sixty years of age. The Club could not in any way have been much better off, having a good bank balance and very good workers for the Club. That year I rode in the 25 miles and I did one hour and twenty minutes, the fastest time that day was just over one hour and eight minutes. I had a twenty minutes start and the winner had eleven minutes start and he rode the 25 miles eleven minutes faster this time and he had the first place with a few seconds. That stopped me having my name on the cup again, I had won the race in 1909. Myself and Mr. Levi were life members, and at that dinner one hundred and fifty sat down. I received my prize for the race, and then the Club made me a splendid presentation of a saw pierced cake basket which they said was for my good work. They had it engraved and I was very pleased with it.

I turned out to nearly all the runs on Thursdays and Sundays. On Sundays I went for an early start and had dinner and returned home for tea. I must mention a few of the fine runs we had – to York every May, leave Tinsley at 5 o'clock for soldiers at York Minster at half past nine. Southwell Cathedral by Ollerton. Bridlington, all night run. Cleethorpes, all night run. Lincoln. Newark. There is one run I shall not forget – in 1926, in my sixtieth year, on Whit. Saturday we met at Plumpers Inn at 12 midnight. I was appointed to lead, I had given orders to ride no more than two abreast and I had fifty cycles following me. The way I went was Blyth, Mattersey, Gainsborough and Caistor. At Caistor, one or two were a little tired and said I had been going too fast, but I was going at one speed which was too much for a few who were not used to that kind of riding.

C.T.C. Jubilee 1928

Cyclists' Touring Club jubilee. That year I was elected to get up a hospital dance. I booked the Cutlers' Hall, that was for twenty-five pounds, and a band ten pounds. I had just over forty pounds to make to pay for the dance, I made it and we had nine pounds for the hospital. When I went to the hospital to tell them I was going to have a C.T.C. jubilee dance and that the balance of the money over the expenses, what a lot of questions were asked. Before I had the bills printed to advertise the dance I went to Dunlop, and they printed them with a small advertisement on the bottom and the C.T.C. Jubilee Dance in large letters. I cycled to every cycle shop in and around Sheffield with bills and tickets, and then cycled around again for the money for tickets sold and returned tickets. When I left a shop on Tinsley Road I was run into with a motor bicycle and sent me flying over the front, I fell between a dray and a motor lorry. A good shaking. The C.T.C. got me five pounds, ten shillings for repairs to my cycle. We had nearly 400 at the dance, and the N.C.U. would not fall in with it. This is the only dance for the hospital the Cyclists' has had and the dinner was overflowing so I was pleased.

1930s holiday rides

These are a few of my holiday runs after the War (First World War) –

GREAT YARMOUTH – rode first day to Kings Lynn, called to look round Sandringham and then did not leave the coast. I stopped at Palling, I was only a few yards from the sea. But what we can learn on these runs, I had a good look at the church, saw how the stones were split in two looking nearly like oyster shells, and Great Yarmouth, a fine place and a fine pier. The fishing boats and the old narrow alleys. I came back through Norwich, Swaffham, and then to Boston and Skegness. LLANDUDNO – first stop at Chester, you want a long stop here for there are a lot of things to see. Then through Holywell, Llandudno and Conway, then turned left for Bettsw-y-Coed. That was a good day's ride. Next day Llanberis and walk up Snowdon and then on to Caernarvon. Went in the castle and then had tea. Next for Llandudno and a look at the Menai Bridge, it is worth seeing. That was another good day. I had a few days in Llandudno, left there at 8 o'clock a.m. and was in the Langsett Road shop at 8 o'clock p.m.

MATLOCK – my first ride was on the ordinary, big wheel, in 1896 and I have been to the same house every year for fifty years.

LONDON – and then to Hatfield for the old-timers' meeting.

LAND'S END – first stop Coventry, second stop Gloucester, fine Cathedral here, next stop Weston-Super-Mare. Then on the coast, Lynmouth. Stop here, you have to see to believe the beauty that the sun sprays. Looked round here. I had a young man riding with me, we got together at Minehead. We had some cider with bread and cheese at an inn with small boulders on the floor and in the middle '1600' was let in. Now this rider, Mr. Bird, was a London gent and he stopped with me at Lynmouth and when I left him at Ilfracombe he invited me to go and see him when I went to London. I called on him, he was an artist and he took me round and I saw what fine work they were doing making pictures for many papers. I had a look round Ilfracombe, my friend was going to Bideford and I stopped at Clovelly, a fine place to look at and saw the donkeys climbing the steep hill. Next stop was Redruth and then round to St. Ives, St. Just to Land's End, Penzance to Falmouth. Next stop was Devonport and Plymouth, two days here then up to Exeter and Taunton, stop here and then through Wells and stop here on my way to Bath. I had a look at Wells Cathedral. Then to Warwick, I took as near a straight line as I could, and from Warwick home. Another grand holiday. I have been to Land's End three times in all.

CORNWALL again – made my ride for Bristol, had a good look round and then for Weston-Super-Mare for night's sleep. Next was a look round

Wells then Glastonbury, Taunton and Exeter. Stopped here for the night, then over Dartmoor, the scenery over the moors was past explaining. I had some long walks and a good dinner at Moreton Hampstead with raspberries and cream for dessert. Then some more up-hills and down-hills, it was a little heavy going for me at my age. I had a look at Princetown and stopped at Tavistock for tea and the night, I was pleased with what I had seen and slept well. Then to Gunnislake where my wife was staying, it was only about four miles from Tavistock. I had two days here, and then on my way. I went down to West Looe, Saltash, Plymouth, Kingsbridge and Dartmouth where I stayed the night. When the man heard I came from Sheffield he asked me if I knew Walter Wragg. I had a good time here and then went to Totnes, a fine old village, Buckfast Abbey and Torquay for one night. Exeter, Honiton, Axminster, Bridport and Dorchester where I had a cup of tea etc. and then went on the lanes, came out at Wareham and stopped at Poole for the night. I took a fine snap of the harbour at sunset. Next to Bournmouth, Christchurch, Lymington and Southampton – took a few good snaps here, I saw the Queen Mary and had a good picture of the ship. Winchester, you could do with a day here to see everything. New Alresford, Alton, Farnham, Aldershot and Bagshot for the night. Made the first left turn for Ascot and Windsor Great Park and Windsor Castle, a look through the fine old building, and then for home.

Scotland

One of the best rides of my life was the one I made to SCOTLAND – first to Glasgow, Dunbarton, Loch Lomond and Tyndrum. After I left Tyndrum going for Glen Coe I had some rough going, it was like slate. This had come down the hills and blocked the roads. I had a sandstorm and a very heavy thunderstorm but I had good shelter at Black Mount shooting boxes and I did have some fine hot sunshine. They had just started to mark out for a new road through the Glen for the motors to get through. At Ballachulish ferry I had to wait a half hour. Fort William, a good tea and a night's rest. Got pally with a gent, and he looked at my cycle, and looked at the transfers and said, "I got one of their catalogues last week." I did not let him know that I was 'Old Smith'. I could see the battleship 'The Hood' on Loch Linnhe. I had a walk with my new friend and had a look up at Ben Nevis. Then for Fort Augustus and Inverness. A fine ride from Fort William to Inverness nearly on Loch Ness, but I did not see the monster! Had a good place for tea, night's rest and breakfast. On the road about 10 o'clock for Dingwall, a flat good road and a fine little place. I went into a shop to buy a few colours (for sketching), the main road turned right between two shops and I came out of the shop and went about five miles the wrong way, and five miles back which made it ten miles, but I had something to look at, old women carrying large baskets on their backs, and old gentlemen in kilts who gave these women money and a smile.

This was at Fodderty. I made for Tain and had lunch here. Six miles from Tain the ferry was about a mile from the road but when I arrived the ferry was not working, so it made it about twenty miles the Bonar Bridge way. I got talking to a young C.T.C. member from London, he said what a grand time he was having. I found a good place at Bonar Bridge, high tea and breakfast with a good supply to have on the road. It was about eighty miles to Wick with some very rough roads. At the top of one hill a sign to look to your brakes and at the bottom two houses whitewashed with stags' skulls with horns on the walls, there looked to be a few hundred of them. Wick, seventeen miles from John O'Groats. When I left John O'Groats to go west, what a wind, I had to stop at Thurso. It was daylight until 12 o'clock, I took a snap at 11 o'clock. I had made my plan to go to the point of Cape Wrath. There is much to see up here, in one village a lot of stone houses were falling down and it looked like only the old people were left for I did not see any young people. They all had a croft, some had a goat and fowls, a few had a cow. I called at a few so-called houses with walls about a yard thick, in one a son on holiday from Canada, he wanted me to stop and for food would not take anything, they said they were so pleased for my being there. But the wind was that strong I was nearly going at walking speed. At Bettyhill I went in the Post Office and sweetshop and a fine looking girl was talking to a man in Gaelic and she asked me if I knew Gaelic, I said I know nobody up here and we had a good laugh. Then I looked to see what was coming, it looked like a family of gypsies in a dirty mess, there seemed to be six women to one man. I had my drink and my sweets and turned to Altnaharra. I lost a lot of the wind now and more downhill. And a good rainstorm – it does rain here when it comes.

Near Altnahar I met a fine old Scot gent. He was at the hotel on the loch side. He advised me to stop at the hotel, and said the landlord would treat me well. I called for tea and asked for bed and breakfast. It was a fine place and they were all gentlemen salmon fishing. Well, I had high tea with silver on the table, a large plate with meat anyone could eat with gravy, and cakes. A fine bedroom with a carpet that was like walking on feathers it was that thick. For breakfast we had porridge and ham and eggs. The landlord came out to wish me well on my way. All this for nine shillings. Down through Lairg, Bonar Bridge, Tain, Dingwall, Inverness to Elgin. It was a Sunday, Scots folk don't like Sunday callers, and there was a bible in every bedroom I stayed at. I found a good place here, at night I was woken up with a circus going through, I was in a front room and had the rumble for over an hour. I had a look round the old abbey etc. Now for Aberdeen, when I arrived it was full up. Hotel in the centre made me a bed in the bathroom, I had high tea and breakfast here for twelve shillings and sixpence. I was keeping to the coast through Stonehaven,

Montrose, Arbroath, Carnoustie to Dundee, and stayed here the night. Old castle and old man-of-war wooden ships were made into offices on the dock side. Tay Bridge – ferry across, Cupar, Leven, Burntisland. Ferry to Edinburgh and met a gent who had a motor on the deck. He talked about London and things that were coming on the market. I had two nights in Edinburgh, there was so much to see. The Forth Bridge must be seen when you are so near, now we see so many things on the pictures it makes a lot of things look second-hand. My next was for Berwick, very old with the old bridge and the new one. I had a bit of hunting for a bed and breakfast but after a while I found one and after tea had a look round, there were a lot of old cannons off old wooden ships. Alnwick, Morpeth and Newcastle, I took a snap of the new bridge they were building, and stayed here for the night. Durham, a fine cathedral and a lot to see here but you must have a guide book. Middlesbrough, Redcar and stopped for the night at Whitby. Pickering and York for the night, and then home. Just over 1,000 miles in fifteen days.

1947

This year, in my 81st year, my total mileage is 3,325. From my 73rd year, that is eight years, I have ridden 32,000 miles. In Sheffield we do not have many people riding cycles at over fifty years of age, they say it is too much like work. Sheffield is in a valley and when we go north we have 500 feet to climb, south 500 feet, east 500 feet, and west over 1,000 feet and with the wind in your face. It may seem a little hard but you have the pleasure of seeing the country and at my time of life after a cycle ride I eat, sleep and feel better, and have all the places I have been to and through to think about. Accidents – I had many falls off the ordinary machine but more recent ones have been – 73 years of age, Manchester Road, freewheeling down with wind at back, motor lorry over crown of road sent me into dust, skidded six yards, caught ground on top of head going over, in hospital three nights, cost me two pounds ten shillings. 79 years of age, Langsett Road, motor lorry out of side street, head hurt, got seventy-five pounds, paid my doctor four pounds ten shillings.

82 year old Herbert Smith riding his 1930s Langsett bicycle in 1948.

Smith family competition medals and certificates

H. Smith

1897		Silver Medal	Yorkshire Road Club, York-Retford T.T.	3hr 5m
19 Aug	1909	Silver Medal	Sheffield Central C.C. Enfield Cup	

E.S. Smith

S. Yorkshire and N. Derbyshire N.C.U., Road Championship 25 miles –

16 June	1923	Bronze Medal	Third	1hr 12m 30 1/5s
31 May	1924	Silver Medal	Second	1hr 7m 48 3/5s

Sheffield Central C.C.

20 June	1924	Silver Medal	Open 25 miles team	1hr 10m 15s
20 July	1924	Bronze Medal	Club 50 miles 3rd h/cap	2hr 31m 49s
20 July	1924	Gold Medal	Club 50 miles Fastest time	2hr 31m 49s
7 May	1925	Certificate	Club 25 miles	1hr 9m 45s
27 June	1925	Certificate	Club Memorial Open 50 miles	2hr 30m 10s
26 July	1925	Certificate	Club 100 miles	5hr 37m 47s
29 May	1926	Certificate	Club Saturday 25 miles	1hr 12m 2s
13 June	1926	Certificate	Club 50 miles	2hr 27m 41s
04 July	1926	Certificate	Club 100 miles	5hr 39m 35s

R.A. Smith

I have no records for R.A. Smith other than Herbert Smith's mention of his winning the Sheffield Central C.C. Telegraph Cup at some time.

Allan Smith's design for the Sheffield Central Cycle Club time trial certificate.
In 1926 he was Race Secretary when Edward Smith was awarded this one.

Frame transfers used on Sheffield Langsett Bicycles

Head or seat tube
1926-1938

Head or seat tube
1939-1962

Seat tube after the
1955 Tour of Britain

Down tube 1926-1935

Down tube 1936

Down tube 1939 cream with black outline – 1952 gold with black outline

Down tube 1956 red with gold
outline or gold with red outline

Top tube 1956

The frame transfers, manufactured in Birmingham by J.W. Beresford & Co. and J.H. Butcher & Co. were fixed by the traditional method with varnish before a final coat of lacquer.

Appendix

Details of all framesets built in the Langsett workshop 1952-1964

The following is the record of all orders and sales of Langsett framesets from 1952-1964, as written in the original order book.

Frame numbers and details are as they are written in the book by Arthur Davidson who was responsible for customer orders. The frame numbers were stamped under the bottom bracket on each frame, but the spacing of the numbers may not necessarily be exactly as recorded in the book. Each frame number relates to the date of order: when ordered each frame was allocated a consecutive serial number, starting at the beginning of each year. This was followed by the number of the month and the year: i.e. 14 3 53 = number 14 of that year ordered March 1953, 921058 = number 92 of that year ordered October 1958. Prefix letters were 'LM' = Langsett Morton (built by Derek Morton), 'P' = Professional, 'C' = Conquest. Although written in the order book these letters were not always stamped on the frame.

Other abbreviations referring to specifications used in the order book are:
M/S = massed start
T.T. = time trial
R = road
P = path
R/P = road/path.

These were not part of the frame number.

1952 FRAMES

NUMBER	ORDER	MODEL	
LM 1/5/52	J. Pound	Special	
LM 2/7/52	Tony Hewson	Special	£12-0-0
LM 3/9/52	Ray Lockwood	Special	£6-6-0
LM 4/10/52	E. Connah		£16-19-6
LM 5/10/52	Spanky McFarlane		£7-10-0
LM 6/10/52	Ken Slater		£12-0-0
LM 7/ /52	shop stock		£16-19-6
LM 8/11/52	A. Hodgson, Leeds	Special	
LM 9/ /52	Terry Nunnington, Sheffield		£16-19-6

1953 FRAMES

NUMBER	ORDER	MODEL	SIZE	COLOUR
LM 1/1/53	shop stock	Professional M/S	24"	Blue
LM 2/1/53	shop stock	Professional T.T.	24"	Blue
LM 3/1/53	shop stock	Professional Path	23"	White
LM 4/1/53	shop stock	Professional M/S	23"	Bronze
LM 5/1/53	shop stock	Professional M/S	23"	Purple
LM 6/1/53	shop stock	Professional T.T.	23"	Blue
LM 7/1/53	shop stock	Professional T.T.	21"	Green
LM 8/2/53	shop stock	Professional M/S	22 ½"	Blue
LM 9/2/53	shop stock	Professional T.T.	22"	Gunmetal
LM 10/2/53	shop stock	Professional M/S	22"	Black
LM 11/2/53	shop stock	Professional M/S	21"	Light gold
LM 12/2/53	shop stock (F.T. Brown)	Professional R/P	23"	Black
LM 13/3/53	Mr. M. McDonald, Barnsley	Professional Road	26"	
LM 14/3/53	Ward Bros.(Finney)	Professional Road	22 ½"	Blue
LM 15/4/53	Mr. Wilson, Sheffield	Professional R/P	22 ½"	Orange
LM 16/4/53	N. Jenkinson	Professional Road	23"	Purple
LM 17/4/53	Ward Bros.	Professional Road	22 ½"	Black
LM 18/5/53	Downend & Lister, Barnsley	Professional Road	24"	Black
LM 19/5/53	Downend & Lister, Barnsley	Professional Road	23"	Chocolate/cream
LM 20/5/53	J. Hardy, Hoyland Common	Professional Path	24"	Black
LM 21/5/53	F. Pintney, Doncaster	Professional Road	23"	Black
LM 22/5/53	F. Pintney, Doncaster	Professional Road	24"	Magenta
LM 23/5/53	Eric Button, Leeds	Professional Road	24 ½"	Ruby red
LM 24/5/53	Mr. Lyne, Sheffield	Professional Road	24"	Green
LM 25/6/53	stock	Professional M/S	21"	Black
LM 26/6/53	stock	Professional M/S	21"	Ruby flam.
LM 27/6/53	stock	Professional M/S	22"	Magenta
LM 28/6/53	stock	Professional M/S	22"	Purple
LM 29/6/53	sold to R. Warwick, Blackburn	Professional M/S	22 ½"	Cambridge/blue
LM 30/6/53	stock	Professional T.T.	23"	Green
LM 31/6/53	stock	Professional M/S	23"	Green
LM 32/6/53	stock	Professional M/S	23"	Black
LM 33/6/53	stock	Professional M/S	23"	Blue flam.
LM 34/6/53	stock	Professional T.T.	23"	Bronze
LM 35/6/53	stock	Professional M/S	23"	Gold
LM 36/6/53	stock	Professional M/S	22 ½"	Blue
LM 37/6/53	stock	Professional M/S	22 ½"	Pink
LM 38/6/53	stock	Professional M/S	23 ½"	Pale blue
LM 39/6/53	stock	Professional M/S	24"	Bronze
LM 40/6/53	stock	Professional M/S	24"	Purple
LM 41/6/53	stock	Professional M/S	24"	Magenta

NUMBER	ORDER	MODEL	SIZE	COLOUR
LM 42/6/53	F.T. Brown, Newcastle, Staffs.	Professional R/P	23"	Black
LM 43/6/53	F.T. Brown, Newcastle, Staffs.	Professional M/S	23"	White
LM 44/6/53	A.E.A. Hodson Cycles, Leeds	Roller racing	22"	Blue
LM 45/6/53	Mercian Cycles, Derby	Professional M/S	23"	Blue
LM 46/6/53	Mercian Cycles, Derby	Professional M/S	22"	Black
LM 47/6/53	C.D. Robson, Manchester	Professional M/S	23"	Green
LM 48/6/53	C.D. Robson, Manchester	Professional M/S	23"	Brown
LM 49/6/53	W. Perrett, Bloxwood, Staffs.	Professional R/P	23"	Black
LM 50/6/53	W. Perrett, (fault – returned)	Professional M/S	22 ½"	Bronze
LM 51/6/53	Eric Button, Leeds	Professional M/S	24 ½"	Ruby
LM 52/7/53	C. Hopkinson, New Whittington	Professional M/S	22"	Blue
LM 53/7/53	C. Hopkinson, New Whittington	Professional M/S		Black/cream
LM 54/8/53	Brian Oxley	Professional M/S	24"	Blue
LM 55/9/53	Foulds, Sheffield	Professional T.T.	22 ½"	Blue
LM 56/9/53	C.D.C. Robson, Manchester	Professional M/S	22"	Green
LM 57/10/53	W.H. Beattie, Middlesbrough	Professional M/S	22 ½"	Blue
LM 57/10/53A	W.H. Beattie, Middlesbrough	Professional M/S	22 ½"	Blue
LM 58/10/53	stock	£12-12-0 model	23 ½"	Lilac
LM 59/10/53	stock	£12-12-0 model	23"	Pale blue
LM 60/10/53	stock	£12-12-0 model	22"	Purple
LM 61/10/53	W. Perrett (in lieu of LM 50)	Professional M/S	22 ½"	Bronze
LM 62/10/53	Quinn Bros., Liverpool	Professional M/S	22 ½"	Bronze
LM 63/10/53	D. Wilson, Sheffield	Professional M/S	23 ½"	Pale green/blue
LM 64/10/53	A. Wilson, Sheffield	Professional M/S	21"	Green/ruby
LM 65/11/53	A. Brough Cycles, Macclesfield	Professional M/S	21 ½"	Bronze/maroon
LM 66/11/53	A. Brough Cycles, Macclesfield	Professional M/S	23 ½"	White/black
LM 67/11/53	M.B. Armstrong, Sheffield	Professional M/S	20"	Purple
LM 68/11/53	W. Perrett Cycles, Bloxwich	Professional Path	23 ½"	Black/cream
LM 69/11/53	R. Grayson, Sheffield	Professional M/S	23"	Black (West St. shop)
LM 70/11/53	M. Spittlehouse, Sheffield	Professional M/S	22 ½"	(West St. shop)
LM 71/11/53	A. Hoyland	Professional M/S	23"	Black (West St. shop)
LM 72/11/53	K. Waby	Professional M/S	23"	Blue (West St. shop)
LM 73/12/53	C.D.C. Robson, Manchester	Professional M/S	23"	Red
LM 74/12/53	C.D.C. Robson, Manchester	Professional M/S	23"	Green
LM 75/12/53	E. Beever, Sheffield	Conquest	23"	Blue
LM 76/12/53	R. Handley (Green Lane works)	Professional M/S		
LM 77/12/53	R. Johnson (Green Lane works)	Professional M/S		
LM 78/12/53	K. Cornthwaite (Infirmary Rd. shop)	Professional M/S		
LM 79/12/53	Robertshaw, Goldthorpe	Professional R/P	23 ½"	Blue
LM 80/12/53	D. Kirk, Sheffield	Professional M/S	21 ½"	Lilac
LM 81/12/53	B. Goodison, Sheffield	Professional M/S	23 ½"	Lilac

1954 FRAMES

NUMBER	ORDER	MODEL	SIZE	COLOUR
LM 1/1/54	stock	Conquest	24"	Blue
LM 2/1/54	stock	Conquest	24"	Maroon
LM 3/1/54	stock	Conquest	24"	Blue
LM 4/1/54	stock	Conquest	24"	
LM 5/1/54	stock	Conquest	24"	
LM 6/1/54	stock	Conquest	24"	
LM 7/1/54	stock	Conquest	24"	
LM 8/1/54	stock	Conquest	24"	
LM 9/1/54	stock	Conquest	21"	
LM 10/1/54	stock	Conquest	21"	
LM 11/1/54	C. Williamson, Doncaster	Conquest	23"	
LM 12/1/54	J. Hall & Son, Blackpool	Conquest	23"	
LM 13/1/54	stock	Conquest	23"	Primer
LM 14/1/54	stock	Conquest	23"	Primer
LM 15/1/54	stock	Conquest	23"	Primer
LM 16/1/54	stock	Conquest	23"	Primer
LM 17/1/54	stock	Conquest	23"	Primer
LM 18/1/54	stock	Conquest	23"	Primer
LM 19/1/54	J. Gill, Sheffield	Professional M/S	22 ½"	(West St. shop)
LM 20/1/54	Dunn, Sheffield	Professional M/S	23 ½"	Bronze
LM 21/1/54	C.C.H. Robson, Manchester	Professional M/S	21 ¾"	Green
LM 22/1/54	C.C.H. Robson, Manchester	Professional M/S	23"	Green
LM 23/1/54	R. Worswich, Blackburn	Professional M/S	23"	Blue
LM 24/1/54	R. Worswich, Blackburn	Conquest	22"	Ruby
LM 25/1/54	Leonard, Sheffield	Conquest	23 ½"	Pink
LM 26/1/54	B.S. Lee, Tankersley	Conquest	22 ½"	Black
LM 27/1/54	J. Hall & Son, Blackpool	Professional M/S	23 ½"	Mauve
LM 28/1/54	C.C.H. Robson, Manchester	Professional	23 ¾"	Duck egg blue
LM 29/2/54	W. Perretts, Bloxwich, Staffs	Conquest	22 ½"	Pale blue
LM 30/2/54	R. Ward, Coal Aston	Professional M/S	23"	Green
LM 31/2/54	Wild, Stocksbridge	Professional R/P	25"	Black
P 32/2/54	June Oliver, Sheffield	Professional M/S	23"	Pink
P 33/2/54	Cowans Cycles, Manchester	Professional M/S	22"	Green flam.
P 34/2/54	Cowans Cycles, Manchester	Professional M/S	23"	Purple flam.
P 35/2/54	Ray Lockwood, Sheffield	Professional R/P	21 ½"	Ruby
P 36/2/54	J. Patching, Bircotes	Professional M/S	24"	Bianchi blue
P 37/2/54	G.B. Reaney, Coal Aston	Professional M/S	22"	Bianchi blue
P 38/3/54	R. Worswich, Blackburn	Professional M/S	22"	Ruby flam.
P 39/3/54	Syd. Turner, Cleveleys	Professional M/S	24"	Ice blue
P 40/3/54	Robertshaw, Goldthorpe	Professional R/P	23 ½"	Blue
P 41/3/54	C.D.C. Robson, Manchester	Professional M/S	23"	Green

NUMBER	ORDER	MODEL	SIZE	COLOUR
P 42/3/54	C.D.C. Robson, Manchester	Professional M/S	23"	Purple flam.
P 43/4/54	A.E.A. Hodson Cycles, Leeds	Professional R/P	21"	Powder blue
P 44/4/54	C.D.C. Robson, Manchester	Professional M/S	23 ¼"	Black/gold
P 45/4/54	A.E. Hodson Cycles, Leeds	Professional	21 ½"	Blue/black
P 46/4/54	P.T. Moss, Leeds	Professional	21 ½"	Black
P 47/4/54	Central Cycle Service, Morecambe	Professional	23"	Green
P 48/5/54	Cowans Cycles, Manchester	Professional	23"	Green
C 49/5/54	Parkin, Sheffield	Conquest	23"	Black
C 50/5/54	Fenwick	Conquest	24"	Black (West St. shop)
C 51/5/54	P.V. Connelly, Sheffield	Conquest	25"	Crimson (West St. shop)
C 52/5/54	Bingham, Rotherham	Conquest	22 ½"	Blue
C 53/5/54	Mr. McGuinness, Sheffield	Conquest	25"	Blue
P 54/5/54	R. Worswich, Blackburn	Professional M/S	23"	Magenta
C 55/5/54	Marsh, Sheffield	Conquest	24"	Black/yellow
C 56/5/54	Johnson, Sheffield	Conquest	26"	White
P 57/6/54	Cowans Cycles, Manchester	Professional M/S	22 ½"	Blue
P 58/6/54	Langston, Sheffield	Professional M/S	23"	Blue
P 59/6/54	York Rally	Professional M/S	22 ½"	Ruby
P 60/7/54	Coldwell, Sheffield	Professional M/S	21"	Mahogany
P 61/7/54	Kitchen, Sheffield	Professional M/S	23"	Duck egg blue
C 62/7/54	stock	Conquest	22"	Primer
C 63/7/54	stock	Conquest	22"	Primer
P 64/7/54	J.T. Rodgers, Leeds	Professional M/S	23"	Black/yellow
C 65/7/54	N. Sullivan (Cycles), Sheffield	Conquest	24"	Black/white
C 66/9/54	stock	Conquest	23"	Primer
C 67/9/54	stock	Conquest	23"	Primer
C 68/9/54	M.J. Heathcote, Sheffield	Conquest	24"	Blue
C 69/9/54	stock	Conquest	24"	Primer
C 70/9/54	stock	Conquest	24"	Primer
C 71/9/54	stock	Conquest	24"	Primer
C 72/9/54	stock	Conquest	24"	Primer
C 73/9/54	stock	Conquest	24"	Primer
P 74/9/54	Badham, Rotherham	Professional	21"	Black
P 75/9/54	Cowans Cycles, Manchester	Professional	22 ½"	Blue
C 76/9/54	stock	Conquest	23"	Primer
C 77/9/54	stock	Conquest	23"	Primer
C 78/9/54	stock	Conquest	23"	Primer
C 79/9/54	stock	Conquest	23"	Primer
C 80/9/54	stock	Conquest	23"	Primer
C 81/11/54	Highgate Cycle Depot, Cleethorpes	Conquest	23"	Blue

NUMBER	ORDER	MODEL	SIZE	COLOUR
C 82/11/54	stock	Conquest path	22"	Primer
C 83/11/54	stock	Conquest path	22 ½"	Primer
C 84/11/54	stock	Conquest path	23 ½"	Primer
P 85/11/54	J.T. Rodgers, Leeds	Professional M/S	24"	Black/white
C 86/11/54	stock	Conquest	22 ½"	Primer
C 87/11/54	stock	Conquest	22 ½"	Primer
C 88/11/54	stock	Conquest	22 ½"	Primer
C 89/11/54	stock	Conquest	24"	Primer
C 90/11/54	stock	Conquest	24"	Primer
C 91/11/54	stock	Conquest	24"	Primer
P 92/11/54	Cowans Cycles, Manchester	Professional	22 ½"	Green
P 93/11/54	Cowans Cycles, Manchester	Professional	22"	Bianchi blue
C 94/11/54	stock	Conquest	24"	Primer
C 95/11/54	stock	Conquest	24"	Primer
C 96/11/54	stock	Conquest	24"	Primer
C 97/11/54	stock	Conquest	24"	Primer
C 98/11/54	stock	Conquest	24"	Primer
C 99/11/54	stock	Conquest	24"	Primer
C 100/11/54	stock	Conquest	24"	Primer
C 101/11/54	stock	Conquest	24"	Primer
C 102/11/54	stock	Conquest	24"	Primer
C 103/11/54	stock	Conquest	24"	Primer

1955 FRAMES

NUMBER	ORDER	MODEL	SIZE	COLOUR
C 1155	stock	Conquest	23 ½"	Primer
C 2155	stock	Conquest	23 ½"	Primer
C 3155	stock	Conquest	23 ½"	Primer
C 4155	stock	Conquest	23 ½"	Primer
C 5155	stock	Conquest	23 ½"	Primer
P 6155	Perrett's Cycle Store, Bloxwich	Professional	22"	Black
P 7155	Perrett's Cycle Store, Bloxwich	Professional	23"	Black
C 8155	H.S. Amy (Cycles), Scunthorpe	Conquest	24"	Black
P 9155	B. Riley, Leeds	Professional	21 ½"	Black
C 10155	H.S. Amy, Highgate Cycles, Cleethorpes	Conquest	23"	Blue
P 11155	J. Slack, Sheffield	Professional	21 ½"	Blue
P 12155	A. South, Sheffield	Professional	21 ½"	Blue
P 13155	J. Pound, Sheffield	Professional Track	21 ½"	Green
P 14155	Highgate Cycles, Scunthorpe	Professional M/S	21"	Blue
P 15155	Dick Bartrop, Sheffield	Professional M/S	23"	
P 16155	H.S. Amy, Highgate Cycles, Cleethorpes	Professional M/S	22"	Egg blue
P 17155	Reg. Browne, Manchester	Professional M/S	23"	Green
P 18155	W. Cowan Cycles, Manchester	Professional M/S	22 ¼"	Green

NUMBER	ORDER	MODEL	SIZE	COLOUR
P 19155	Shaw, Sheffield	Professional M/S	23"	Ruby
P 20155	Cowans Cycles, Manchester	Professional M/S	22 ½"	Green
C 21155	Highgate Cycles, Cleethorpes	Conquest	23"	Light blue
P 22255	Colin Tidd, Dronfield	Professional	22 ½"	Powder blue
P 23255	B. Clayton, Rotherham	Professional	22 ½"	Black
P 24255	Cowans Cycles, Manchester	Professional	24"	Eau de Nil
P 25355	Cowans Cycles, Manchester	Professional	23"	Blackcurrant
P 26355	W. Perrett Cycles, Bloxwich	Professional	24"	Black
P 27355	A.E.A. Hodson Cycles, Leeds	Professional Path	22"	Black
P 28355	A.E.A. Hodson Cycles, (P.J. Moss)	Professional Path	21"	White
P 29355	W.H. Beatie, Middlesbrough	Professional M/S	23"	Blue
P30455	W.G. Jackson, Rotherham	Professional M/S	23"	Blue
P 31455	Cowans Cycles, Manchester	Professional	21 ¼"	Green
C 32455	stock	Conquest	25"	Pale blue
P 33455	Robinson, Sheffield	Professional	21"	Black
C 34455	Cowans Cycles, Manchester	Conquest	22"	Purple
C 35455	Highgate Cycles, Cleethorpes	Conquest	24 ½"	Pink
P 36555	R. Mottram, Sheffield	Professional	22"	Blue
P 37655	Mick Waterfield	Professional	23 ½"	Blue
P 38655	Tony Hewson, Sheffield	Professional	23 ½"	Blue
P 39655	J. Short, Sheffield	Professional	23"	Blue
P 40655	E. Wheen, Sheffield	Professional	22"	Blue
P 41655	Highgate Cycles, Cleethorpes	Professional	23"	Pink
C 42655	J. Leversidge, Sheffield	Conquest	25"	Blue
P 43655	Cowans Cycles, Manchester	Professional	23"	Green
P 44655	stock – York Rally	Professional	22 ½"	Black
P 45755	stock – York Rally	Professional Junior	16"	Ruby
P 46755	stock – York Rally	Professional	23"	
P 47755	Cowans Cycles, Manchester	Professional	23"	Ruby
C 48855	Siddall, (Cycles), Rotherham	Conquest	22"	Black
P 49855	T. Nunnington, Sheffield	Professional	22 ³/₁₆"	Green
P 50855	Spanky McFarlane, Sheffield	Professional	20 ¾"	Orange flam.
P 51855	B.H. Verity, Leeds (going to Australia)	Professional Path	24"	Black
P 52855	Regent Cycle Stores, Nelson, Lancs	Professional	24 ½"	Black
P 53955	Cowans Cycles (Reg. Browne)	Professional	23"	Pink
C 54955	Bev Wood, Droylesden, Lancs.	Conquest	23"	White
P 551055	J. Williams, Wolverhampton	Professional	22 ½"	Pink/green
P 561055	B. Taylor, (West St. shop)	Professional	22"	Blue
P 571055	G. Lilley, Rotherham	Professional Path	22 ½"	
P 581055	Horton & Hollinder, Wetherby	Professional Path	22"	White
P 591055	Brough Cycles, Macclesfield	Professional		Mushroom/red
P 601055	J. Pound, Sheffield	Professional	21"	Yellow
C 611155	N. Sullivan (Cycles), Sheffield	Conquest	26"	Green
C 621055	stock – J. Kingston	Conquest	23"	Purple
C 631055	Bev Wood, Droylesden, Lancs.	Conquest	23"	Duck egg

NUMBER	ORDER	MODEL	SIZE	COLOUR
P 641055	Cowans Cycles, Manchester	Professional	22 ½"	Bianchi blue
P 651155	Leedham & Son, Leicester	Professional	24"	Grey/maroon
P 661155	W. Staniforth, Sheffield	Professional	24"	Ruby/black
P 671155	D. Harrison, Hull	Professional	23"	Blue/red
P 681155	F. Williams, Wolverhampton	Professional	23"	Ruby/black
P 691155	A. Geddis Cycles, Belfast	Professional	23"	Green/yellow
C 701155	A. Geddis Cycles, Belfast	Conquest	23"	Red
C 711155	A. Geddis Cycles, Belfast	Conquest	22"	Blue
P 721255	Mick Waterfield, Sheffield	Professional	23 ½"	Blue
P 731255	J. Cressey, Sheffield	Professional	23"	Black
P 741255	June Thackray, Sheffield	Professional	23"	
P 751255	G. Evans, Leicester	Professional	23"	Blue
P 761255	G. Lilley, Rotherham	Professional Path	22 ½"	Ruby
C 771255	J.K. Carter, Hull	Conquest	23"	Blue
C 781255	Bev Wood, Droylesden, Lancs	Conquest	22 ½"	Black
C 791255	A.E. Butterworth Cycles, Sheff.	Conquest	22"	Blue
C 801255	H.S. Amy, Cleethorpes	Conquest	24"	Black
P 811255	A.E. Hodson, Leeds	Professional Path	21 ½"	Blue
C 821255	E.C. Johnson, Ormskirk	Conquest	23"	Green

1956 FRAMES

NUMBER	ORDER	MODEL	SIZE	COLOUR
P 1156	Jack Kirk, Hull	Professional	22"	Cream
P 2156	T. Simpson, Doncaster	Professional	22 ½"	Ruby flam.
P 3156	D. Alcock, Sheffield	Professional	22 ¼"	Blue
C 4156	H. Child, Hull	Conquest	24"	Green
P 5156	Ellis Cycle Stores, Oswestry	Professional	23"	Kingfisher
C 6156	Colin Tidd, Dronfield	Conquest	24 ½"	Blue
P 7156	Bev Wood, Droylesden, Lancs.	Professional	22 ½"	Blue
P 8156	R. Telford, Sheffield	Professional	21 ½"	Green
P 9156	C.D.C. Robson, Manchester	Professional	24 ½"	Black
C 10156	C.D.C. Robson, Manchester	Conquest	23"	Green
C 11156	E. Ellis, Sheffield	Conquest	22"	Purple
C 12256	W. Siddall Cycles, Rotherham	Conquest	22"	Black
P 13256	W.H. Sharp, Worksop	Professional	19 ½"	Bianchi blue
C 14256	stock	Conquest	22"	Primer
C 15256	stock	Conquest	23"	Primer
C 16256	stock	Conquest	23"	Primer
C 17256	stock	Conquest	23"	Primer
C 18256	stock	Conquest	23"	Primer
C 19256	stock	Conquest	23"	Primer
C 20256	stock	Conquest	23"	Primer
C 21256	stock	Conquest	23"	Primer
C 22256	stock	Conquest	23"	Primer
C 23256	stock	Conquest	23"	Primer
C 24256	stock	Conquest	23"	Primer
C 25256	stock	Conquest	23"	Primer
P 26256	Cowans Cycles, Manchester	Professional	22"	Blue

NUMBER	ORDER	MODEL	SIZE	COLOUR
P 27256	Brough's, Macclesfield	Professional	21"	Pink
P 28356	Don Wilson, Hull	Professional	21 ½"	Silver/red
C 29356	stock	Conquest	22"	Bianchi blue
C 30356	Leedham & Son, Leicester	Conquest	24"	Green
P 31356	A.E. Hodson, Leeds (D. Simpson)	Professional Path	22"	Kingfisher
P 32356	A.E. Hodson, Leeds (R. Franklin)	Professional Path	21"	Blue
C 33356	Bev Wood, Droylesden, Lancs	Conquest	25"	White
P 34356	Cowans Cycles, Manchester	Professional	23 ½"	Ruby flam.
C 35356	W.H. Sharp & Son, Worksop	Conquest	20 ½"	Pink
C 36456	Leedham & Son, Leicester	Conquest	24"	Black
C 37456	stock	Conquest	22"	Bianchi blue
C 38456	W. Siddall (Cycles), Rotherham	Conquest	22"	Black
P 39456	stock	Professional	22"	Ruby
P 40456	stock	Professional	22"	Bianchi blue
P 41456	stock	Professional	23"	Green
P 42456	stock	Professional	23"	Black
P 43456	stock	Professional	23"	Blue
P 44456	stock	Professional	24"	Kingfisher
C 45456	D. Ryalls, Sheffield	Conquest	22 ½"	Blue
C 46556	W. Siddall (Cycles), Rotherham	Conquest	22"	Black
C 47556	A.E. Butterworth Cycles, Sheffield	Conquest	22"	Ruby
C 48556	A.E. Butterworth Cycles, Sheffield	Conquest	23"	Bianchi blue
C 49556	Bev Wood, Droylesden, Lancs.	Conquest	21"	Black
C 50556	W.G. Maples Cycles, Lincoln	Conquest	22 ½"	Purple
P 51556	Cowans Cycles, Manchester	Professional	23"	Pink
P 52556	Cowans Cycles, Manchester	Professional	22 ½"	Purple flam.
P 53556	B. Simpson, Sheffield	Professional	22 ½"	Blue
P 54556	Tony Hewson	Professional	23 ½"	Duck egg blue
P 55556	A.E. Hodson, Leeds (D. Simpson)	Professional Path	22"	Kingfisher
C 56556	R. Levers, Sheffield	Conquest	21 ½"	Black
P 57556	J. Simpson, Doncaster	Professional Path	23"	Ruby
C 58556	W. Jackson, Sheffield	Conquest	23"	Ruby
C 59556	C.D.C. Robson, Manchester	Conquest	22 ½"	Black
P 60556	Jack Kirk Ltd., Hull	Professional	24"	Peach
P 61556	P. Ellis, South Anston	Professional	23"	Black
P 62556	W.G. Maples Cycles, Lincoln	Professional	23 ½"	Blue
C 63656	W. Binns, Castleford	Conquest	23"	Grey
P 64656	J. Hall & Son, Blackpool	Professional	22"	Blue
C 65656	A.E. Butterworth Cycles, Sheffield	Conquest	22"	Black
C 66656	A.E. Butterworth Cycles, Sheffield	Conquest	22"	Black
P 67756	Economic Radio Ltd., Pontefract	Professional	24"	White
C 68756	W.G. Maples Cycles, Lincoln	Conquest	22 ½"	Old rose

NUMBER	ORDER	MODEL	SIZE	COLOUR
C 69756	stock	Conquest	24"	Primer
C 70756	stock	Conquest	24"	Primer
C 71756	stock	Conquest	24"	Primer
C 72756	stock	Conquest	24"	Primer
C 78756	stock	Conquest	24"	Primer
C 79756	stock	Conquest	22"	Primer
C 80756	stock	Conquest	22"	Primer
C 81756	stock	Conquest	22"	Primer
C 82756	stock	Conquest	22"	Primer
C 83756	stock	Conquest	22"	Primer
C 84756	stock	Conquest	22"	Primer
C 85756	stock	Conquest	22"	Primer
C 86756	stock	Conquest	22"	Primer
C 87756	stock	Conquest	22"	Primer
C 88756	stock	Conquest	22"	Primer
C 89756	stock	Conquest	21"	Primer
C 90756	stock	Conquest	21"	Primer
C 91756	stock	Conquest	21"	Primer
P 92856	Brough's Cycles, Macclesfield	Professional	24"	Mushroom
P 93856	W.G. Maples Cycles, Lincoln	Professional	22"	Ruby
P 94856	Mr. McNally, Sheffield	Professional	25"	Ruby
C 95856	Leedham & Son, Leicester	Conquest	24"	Grey
C 96856	Highgate Cycles, Cleethorpes	Conquest	23"	Red
C 97856	W. Siddall (Cycles), Rotherham	Conquest	20"	Magenta
P 98856	W. Perret (Cycles), Bloxwich	Professional Path	24"	Blue
C 99956	Mr. Lyne, Sheffield	Conquest	24"	Blue
P 100956	Bev Wood, Droylesden, Lancs	Professional	23"	Blue
P 101956	A.E. Hodson, Leeds	Professional Path	21 ¾"	Beige
C 102956	Leedham & Son, Leicester	Conquest	23"	Grey/green
P 1031056	W.G. Maples Cycles, Lincoln	Professional	21"	Ruby
P 1041056	A.C. Mundy, Peterborough	Professional	24"	White
P 1051056	Cowan's Cycles, Manchester	Professional	23"	Purple
P 1061156	B. Frost, Normanton, Yorks.	Professional	22"	Gunmetal
P 1071156	N. Griffin, Lincoln	Professional	23 ½"	Pale blue
P 1081156	C.D.C. Robson, Manchester	Professional	21 ¼"	Ice blue
P 1091256	W.G. Maples Cycles, Lincoln	Professional	24"	Pink
C 1101256	C.D.C. Robson, Manchester	Conquest	24"	Black

1957 FRAMES

NUMBER	ORDER	MODEL	SIZE	COLOUR
P 1157	P. Brown, Sheffield	Professional	23 ½"	Blue
P 2157	K.B. Lycett, Pontefract	Professional	21"	Blue
C 3157	B. Beresford, Sheffield	Conquest	22"	Ruby
C 4157	George Rayner & Son, Scunthorpe	Conquest	22"	Pink
C 5157	George Rayner & Son, Scunthorpe	Conquest	23"	Black
C 6157	C.D.C. Robson, Manchester	Conquest	21 ½"	Orange

NUMBER	ORDER	MODEL	SIZE	COLOUR
P 7157	C.D.C. Robson, Manchester	Professional	20"	Blue
P 8157	G. Newey, Sheffield	Professional	22"	Blue
C 9157	W. Stacey, Sheffield	Conquest	24"	Ruby
P 10157	J. Hall, Sheffield	Professional	25"	Mushroom
P 11157	Haigh, Sheffield	Professional	22 ½"	Blue
P 12157	W.A. Bentall, Sheffield	Professional	24"	Black
P 13157	Denton Cycles, Newcastle on Tyne	Professional	22"	Green
P 14257	Brough's Cycles, Macclesfield	Professional	21"	Blue
P 15257	W.G. Maples Cycles, Lincoln	Professional	24"	Pink
P 16257	Jack Kirk Ltd., Hull	Professional	23 ½"	Blue
P 17257	Jack Kirk Ltd., Hull	Professional	22 ½"	Blue
P 18257	D. Orford, Ambergate	Professional	23"	Blue
P 19257	J. Bennett, Derby	Professional	22"	Blue
P 20257	H. Gould, Derby	Professional	23 ½"	Blue
P 21257	B. Trippett, Sheffield	Professional	21"	Blue
P 22257	P. Ryalls, Sheffield	Professional	22"	Blue
P 23257	A. Hoyland, Sheffield	Professional	23"	Blue
P 24257	W & R Baines, Bradford	Professional	23"	Blue
C 25257	Cliff Pratt, Hull	Conquest	23"	Eau de Nil
P 26257	R. Ironside, Sheffield	Professional	24"	Grey
P 27257	W. Woods, Sheffield	Professional	22"	Ruby
P 28257	W. Moyes, Edinburgh	Professional	22"	Blue
P 29357	F. Brookes, Rotherham	Professional	24"	
C 30357	G. Rayner & Son, Scunthorpe	Conquest	22 ½"	Black
C 31357	W. Siddall (Cycles), Rotherham	Conquest Path	22 ½"	Blue
P 32357	A.E. Hodson, Leeds	Professional Path	22"	Lilac
P 33357	R. Pearson, Sunderland, Co. Durham	Professional	23"	Maroon
C 34357	N.S. Sullivan Ltd., Sheffield	Conquest	24 ½"	Citrus yellow
C 35457	Mr. J.F. Mugglestone, Retford	Conquest	22"	Black
P 36457	Bev Wood, Droylesden, Lancs.	Professional	23"	Blue
P 37457	J. O'Neill, Sheffield	Professional	23"	Grey
P 38457	Bev Wood, Droylesden, Lancs.	Professional	23"	Blue
P 39457	Horton & Hollinder, Wetherby	Professional	23 ½"	Blue
C 40457	G. Rayner & Son, Scunthorpe	Conquest	22"	Blue
P 41457	T.A. Goddard, Sheffield	Professional	22 ½"	Black
C 42457	C.D.C. Robson, Manchester	Conquest	23 ½"	Grey
P 43557	Denton Cycles, Newcastle on Tyne	Professional	22"	Black
C 44557	N.S. Sullivan Ltd., Sheffield	Conquest	24"	Black
C 45557	N.S. Sullivan Ltd., Sheffield	Conquest	24"	Black
C 46557	Bev Wood, Droylesden, Lancs.	Conquest	24"	Gold
C 47557	Cliff Pratt, Hull	Conquest	23"	Eau de Nil
C 48557	Cliff Pratt, Hull	Conquest	22 ½"	Ice blue
P 49557	Frank Short, Sheffield	Professional	23"	Orange
C 50557	N.S. Sullivan Ltd., Sheffield	Conquest	24 ½"	Black

NUMBER	ORDER	MODEL	SIZE	COLOUR
P 51557	J. Harris, Doncaster	Professional	21 ½"	Blue
P 52657	Mulryan, Sheffield	Professional	23 ½"	Blue
C 53657	Cliff Pratt, Hull	Conquest	22"	Blue
P 54657	Wride, Sheffield	Professional	22"	Blue
P 55757	A.E. Hodson, Leeds	Professional	21 ½"	Blue
C 56757	Cliff Pratt, Hull	Conquest	23"	Blue
C 57757	J.A. Webster Cycles, Chesterfield	Conquest	23"	Blue
P 58757	S.B. Harrison, Sheffield	Professional	26"	Black
C 59757	J. Harris, Doncaster	Conquest	22"	Black
C 60757	stock	Conquest	23"	
C 61757	stock	Conquest	23"	
C 62757	stock	Conquest	23"	
C 63757	stock	Conquest	23"	
C 64757	stock	Conquest	23"	
C 65757	stock	Conquest	23"	
C 66757	stock	Conquest	23"	
C 67757	stock	Conquest	23"	
C 68757	stock	Conquest	23"	
C69757	stock	Conquest	23"	
C 70757	stock	Conquest	23"	
P 71757	P. Flintham, Rotherham	Professional	24"	Ruby
P 72857	W.G. Maples Cycles, Lincoln	Professional	22 ½"	Ruby
P 73857	Tony Burgess, Stockport	Professional	25"	Grey
C 74857	Bev Wood, Droylesden, Lancs.	Conquest	24"	Black
P 75857	Wride, Sheffield	Professional	22"	Honeysuckle
P 76857	Haigh, Sheffield	Professional	25"	Green
C 77957	N.S. Sullivan Ltd., Sheffield	Conquest	23"	Black
C 78957	N.S. Sullivan Ltd., Sheffield	Conquest	23"	Blue
C 791057	W.G. Maples Cycles, Lincoln	Conquest	24 ½"	Black
C 801057	Gallagher, Sheffield	Conquest	22"	Blue
P 811057	Bev Wood, Droylesden, Lancs.	Professional	22 ½"	Purple
P 821057	P.J. Huckstepp, Sheffield	Professional	23 ½"	Blue
P 831057	G. Shaw, Sheffield	Professional	23"	Orange
C 841157	E. Barber, Sheffield	Conquest	23"	Blue
C 851157	T.J. Sylvester, Lincoln	Conquest Path	21 ½"	Ivory
C 861157	N.S. Sullivan Ltd., Sheffield	Conquest	20"	Black
P 871157	A.J. Millington, Stoke-onTrent	Professional	24"	Mushroom
C 881157	A. Geddis (Cycles), Belfast	Conquest	20 ½"	Beige
P 891157	Finnie's, Edinburgh	Professional	24"	Green
P 901157	J.R.J. Cycles Ltd., Leeds	Professional	22 ¼"	Blue
P 911157	Alan South, Sheffield	Professional	23"	Orange
C 921257	W. Siddall (Cycles), Rotherham	Conquest	20"	Green
C 931257	stock	Conquest	22"	Ruby
P 941257	stock	Professional	22"	Black
C 951257	stock	Conquest Path	22 ½"	Red

1958 FRAMES

NUMBER	ORDER	MODEL	SIZE	COLOUR
C 1158	stock	Conquest	22"	Black
2158	stock	Conquest	22"	Ruby
3158	stock	Conquest	22"	Blue
4158	stock	Conquest	22"	Grey
5158	stock	Conquest	22"	Black
6158	A.E. Butterworth Cycles, Sheffield	Conquest	23"	Red
7158	A.E. Butterworth Cycles, Sheffield	Conquest	23"	Mushroom
8158	A.E. Butterworth Cycles, Sheffield	Conquest	23"	Blue
9158	B. Tompkin, Sheffield	Conquest	23"	Black
10158	stock	Conquest	23"	Grey
11158	Ellis, Sheffield	Professional	23"	Green
12158	Denton Cycles, Newcastle on Tyne	Professional	22"	Red
13158	Jack Kirk Ltd., Hull	Professional R/P	23"	Blue
14158	Jack Kirk Ltd., Hull	Professional R/P	22 ½"	Ruby
15158	F.R. Russell, Walsall	Professional R/P	24"	Black
16158	J. Beal, Sheffield	Professional	22 ½"	Mushroom
17158	Perret Cycles, Bloxwich	Professional R/P	23 ½"	Black
18158	Jack Kirk Ltd., Hull	Conquest	22"	Blue
19158	Norman Sullivan Ltd., Sheffield	Professional	24"	Black
20158	G. Raynor, Scunthorpe	Conquest R/P	23"	Black
21258	Leedham & Son, Leicester	Conquest	22 ½"	Grey
22258	A. Geddis Cycles, Belfast	Conquest	21"	Lime green
23258	A.E. Hodson Cycles, Leeds	Professional Path		Green
24258	D. Wilson, Sheffield	Professional	23 ½"	Ruby
25258	A. Geddis Cycles, Belfast	Professional	22"	Ruby
26258	Bache Bros., Stourbridge	Professional	23 ½"	Orange/blue
27258	M.S. Hayes, Boston, Lincs.	Conquest R/P	22 ½"	
28258	P. Booth, Sheffield	Professional	22"	Red
29258	Denton Cycles, Newcastle on Tyne	Professional	22"	Red/yellow
30258	Jack Kirk Ltd., Hull	Professional R/P		Blue
31258	stock	Professional	23"	Ruby
32258	stock	Conquest	24"	Blue
33258	Read, Sheffield	Conquest	24"	Black
34358	stock	Conquest R/P	22"	Black
35358	stock	Conquest R/P	22 ½"	Orange
36358	stock	Conquest R/P	23"	Green
37358	P. Crawford, Sheffield	Professional	22 ½"	Red
38358	E.J. Kilner, Clowne	Conquest	23"	Blue
39358	Perrett Cycles, Bloxwich	Conquest R/P	23"	Blue
40358	Elliston, Sheffield	Conquest	24"	Maroon

NUMBER	ORDER	MODEL	SIZE	COLOUR
41358	A.E. Hodson Cycles, Leeds	Professional	23"	Green
42358	A.E. Hodson Cycles, Leeds	Professional Path	22 ½"	Green
43358	A.E. Hodson Cycles, Leeds	Conquest	21 ½"	Beige
44358	J.A. Webster Cycles, Chesterfield	R/P	23"	Magenta
45358	J.A. Webster Cycles, Chesterfield	Conquest	24"	Grey
46358	J.A. Webster Cycles, Chesterfield	R/P	23"	Green
47358	Leedham & Son, Leicester	Conquest	25"	Blue
48358	Tony Burgess, Stockport	Professional	23"	Grey
49458	A. Geddis Cycles, Belfast	R/P	22"	Blue
50458	Matt Newton Ltd., Middlesbrough	Conquest		Grey
51458	P. Rutter, Sheffield	Professional	22"	Blue
52458	Norman Sullivan Ltd., Sheffield	Professional	25"	Black
53458	Bill Hurst, Hindley, Lancs.	Professional	23"	Copper
54458	J. Needham, Sheffield	Professional	25"	Blue
55458	G. Finn, Sheffield	Professional	22 ½"	Orange
56458	W.H. Millington, Ossett	Professional	24"	Blue
57458	Horton & Hollinder, Wetherby	Conquest R/P	23"	Blue
58558	Norman Sullivan Ltd., Sheffield	Professional	24"	Blue
59558	David Forbes, San Francisco, USA	Conquest	23 ½"	Ivory
60558		Professional	23"	Purple
61558	Leedham & Son, Leicester	Conquest	22"	Grey
62558	Horton & Hollinder, Wetherby	Conquest	24"	Grey
63558	J.D. Croft, Sheffield	Conquest	24"	Black
64558	A.J. Blackwell, Rotherham	Conquest	21"	Copper
65558	A.C. Mundy, Peterborough	Professional	23"	Blue
66658	Joe Marsh, Manchester	R/P	23"	Black
67658	Matt Newton Ltd., Middlesbrough	Conquest	21"	Grey
68658	Matt Newton Ltd., Middlesbrough	Conquest	23"	Blue
69658	Matt Newton Ltd., Middlesbrough	Conquest	23"	Grey
70658	Leedham & Son, Leicester	Conquest R/P	25"	Mauve
71658	A. Geddis Cycles, Belfast	Conquest R/P	22"	Red
72658	stock – York Rally	Conquest R/P	22 ½"	Orange
73658	stock – York Rally	Conquest M/S	22 ½"	Green
74658	stock – York Rally	Conquest M/S	23"	Blue
75658	stock – York Rally	Professional M/S	23"	Copper
76658	F. Holden, Marple, Cheshire	Conquest M/S	23"	Wine red
77658	F. Holden, Marple, Cheshire	Professional M/S	23"	Black
78658	A.J. Blackwell, Rotherham	Conquest M/S	23"	Black
79658	Norman Sullivan Ltd., Sheffield	Professional M/S	24"	Yellow
80658	Perrett Cycles, Bloxwich	Professional	23"	Pink

NUMBER	ORDER	MODEL	SIZE	COLOUR
81758	B.T.C. (Marlow)	Professional	23"	Mauve
82758	Norman Sullivan Ltd., Sheffield	Conquest	24"	Black
83858	W.G. Maples Cycles, Lincoln	Professional Path	22 ½"	Maroon
84858	M. Bedford, Barnsley (Compton)	Conquest R/P		Black
85858	Bev Wood, Droylesden, Lancs.	Professional	24"	Yellow
86958	Norman Sullivan Ltd., Sheffield	Conquest R/P	24"	Ruby
87958	C. Taylor, Doncaster	Professional M/S	23"	Ruby
88958	W.G. Maples Cycles, Lincoln	Conquest R/P	22"	Red
89958	Matt Newton Ltd., Middlesbrough	Conquest	22"	Silver
90958	Matt Newton Ltd., Middlesbrough	Conquest	23"	Ruby
91958	G. Bradshaw, Sheffield	Conquest R/P	22"	Red
921058	Denton Cycles, Newcastle on Tyne	Professional	22 ½"	Ruby
931058	Norman Sullivan Ltd., Sheffield	Conquest R/P	23"	Blue
941058	Norman Sullivan Ltd., Sheffield	Conquest R/P	22"	Ruby
951058	L.H. Dodd, Sheffield	Professional M/S	19 ¾"	Orange
961158	M. Selwood, Rawmarsh	Conquest	25"	Blue
971158	Brampton Cycles, Chesterfield	Professional	24"	Grey
981158	J. Hutchins, Leeds	Conquest R/P	23"	Red
991158	Matt Newton Ltd., Middlesbrough	Conquest	24"	Blue
1001258	J.R.J. Cycles, Leeds	Professional	24"	Lilac

1959 FRAMES

NUMBER	ORDER	MODEL	SIZE	COLOUR
1159	Jack Kirk Ltd., Hull	Professional	22"	Red
2159	Highgate Cycles, Cleethorpes	Professional	23"	Blue
3159	Leedham & Son, Leicester	Conquest	23"	Black
4159	Joe Marsh, Manchester	Conquest	23"	Copper flam.
5159	Joe Marsh, Manchester	Conquest	23"	Red
6159	F.R. Russell, Walsall	Professional	23"	Blue
7159	Bob Roote, Scarborough	Professional	22"	Green
8159	(In place of 981158)	Conquest R/P	23"	Red
9159	Trevor Goddard, Sheffield	Professional	24 ½"	Red
10259	Jim Broome, Salford	Professional	22"	Ruby
11259	Wm. Moyes, Edinbugh	Professional	23 ½"	Grey
12259	Wm. Moyes, Edinbugh	Professional	21 ½"	Orange
13259	C.P. Oldham, Sheffield	Conquest	24 ½"	Orange
14259	stock	Conquest	23"	Blue
15259	Norman Sullivan Ltd., Sheffield	Professional	24"	Orange
16259	stock	Professional	23"	Ruby

NUMBER	ORDER	MODEL	SIZE	COLOUR
17259	Bev Wood, Droylesden, Lancs	Professional	23"	Purple
18259	Bev Wood, Droylesden, Lancs	Professional	24"	Pink
19259	Jack Kirk, Hull	Conquest	24"	Blue
20259	W.S. Maples Cycles, Lincoln	Conquest	21"	Green
21259	A. Lees, Manchester	Professional	23"	Grey
22259	Brampton Cycles, Chesterfield	Conquest	23"	Green
23259	E. Yarrow, Sunderland	Professional	25 ½"	White
24259	G. Raynor & Son, Scunthorpe	Conquest R/P		Grey
25359	D. Organer, Lincoln	Professional	24"	Ruby
26359	M. Woodcock, Leeds	Professional	24"	Blue
27359	Barry Lomas, Staffordshire	Conquest	24"	Pink
28359	Leedham & Son, Leicester	Conquest	24"	Black
29359	Wallis Cycles, Scarborough	Professional	22"	Maroon
30359	A. Williamson, Stockport	Professional	22"	
31359	M. Coupe, Sheffield	Professional	24"	
32359	Keith Lyne, Sheffield	Professional	24"	
33459	Barker, Wentworth, Rotherham	Conquest	24"	Black
34459	stock	Conquest	23"	
35459	stock	Conquest	23"	
36459	stock	Conquest	23"	
37459	stock	Conquest	23"	
38459	stock	Conquest	23"	
39459	stock	Conquest	23"	
40459	stock	Conquest	23"	
41459	stock	Conquest	23"	
42459	stock	Conquest	23"	
43459	stock	Conquest	23"	
44459	Norman Sullivan Ltd., Sheffield	Conquest	24"	Black
45459	Norman Sullivan Ltd., Sheffield	Conquest	24"	Orange
46459	stock	Conquest	23"	
47459	stock	Conquest	23"	
48459	D. Richardson, Hessle, E. Yorks.	Conquest	24"	Green
49559	W. Siddall Cycles, Rotherham	Conquest	24"	Black
50559	J.A. Webster Cycles, Chesterfield	Conquest	24"	Grey
51559	F. Holden, Marple, Cheshire	Conquest	22"	Red
52559	J. Kelly, Stocksbridge, Sheffield	Conquest	25"	Blue
53559	A. Doyle, Oldham	Professional	20"	Silver
54559	Norman Sullivan Ltd., Sheffield	Conquest	23"	Orange
55559	Norman Sullivan Ltd., Sheffield	Conquest	23"	Blue
56559	Norman Sullivan Ltd., Sheffield	Conquest	23"	Black
57559	R. Green, Leeds	Professional	21"	Black
58659	Solo Cycles, Peterborough	Conquest	23"	Orange

NUMBER	ORDER	MODEL	SIZE	COLOUR
59659	W.S. Maples Cycles, Lincoln	Conquest	23"	Green
60659	A.E. Butterworth Cycles, Sheff.	Professional	24"	Orange
61659	M. Shirley, Sheffield	Professional	23 ½"	Silver
62759	W. Siddalls Cycles, Rotherham	Professional	25"	White
63759	Solo Cycles, Peterborough	Conquest R/P	21"	Blue
64759	Solo Cycles, Peterborough	Conquest	23"	Orange
65759	C.D. Robson Cycles, Manchester	Conquest	20 ½"	Green
66759	J. Hepworth, Sheffield	Conquest	19 ½"	Red
67759	J.A. Webster Cycles, Chesterfield	Conquest	24"	Blue
68759	J.S. Greaves, Sheffield	Professional	23"	Green
69759	Bev Wood, Droylesden, Lancs.	Professional	24"	Purple
70759	J.N. Jackson, Woodhouse	Professional	25"	Blue
71859	D. Pawley, Sheffield	Professional	23"	Red
72859	Norman Sullivan Ltd., Sheffield	Conquest	21"	Black
73959	W. Perrett Cycles, Bloxwich	Professional Path	23 ½"	Grey
74959	W.S. Maples Cycles, Lincoln	Professional	24"	Pewter
751059	C.D. Robson Cycles, Manchester	Conquest	24"	Black
761059	stock	Conquest	22"	Black
771059	A. Boyle, Sheffield	Conquest	21 ½"	Silver
781059	stock	Conquest	23"	
791059	stock	Conquest	23"	
801059	stock	Conquest	23"	
811059	stock	Conquest	23"	
821059	stock	Conquest	23"	
831059	stock	Conquest	23"	
841059	stock	Conquest	24"	
851059	stock	Conquest	24"	
861059	stock	Conquest	24"	
871059	Marriott, Sheffield	Professional	22"	Blue
881059	Denton Cycles, Newcastle on Tyne	Professional	23"	White
891059	Matt Newton Ltd., Middlesbrough	Professional	23"	Copper flam.
901159	M.A. James Cycles, Alford	Professional	22"	Red
911159	M.A. James Cycles, Alford	Conquest	22"	Blue
921159	Denton Cycles, Newcastle on Tyne	Professional	22"	Black
931159	Miss Johnson, Barnsley	Conquest	19 ½"	Green
941159	Norman Sullivan Ltd., Sheffield	Professional	24"	Lilac
951159	Norman Sullivan Ltd., Sheffield	Conquest	21"	Ruby
961159	Pete Hampson, Sheffield	Professional	23"	Ruby
971159	Roger Macrae Cycles, Edinburgh	Professional	22"	Bronze
981259	Norman Sullivan Ltd., Sheffield	Conquest	23"	Orange

NUMBER	ORDER	MODEL	SIZE	COLOUR
991259	Jack Kirk Ltd., Hull	Conquest	23"	Green
1001259	D. Richardson, Hessle, E.Yorks	Conquest	24"	Eau de Nil

1960 FRAMES

NUMBER	ORDER	MODEL	SIZE	COLOUR
1160	A. Geddis Cycles, Belfast	Conquest	22 ½"	Black
2160	Bev Wood, Droylesden, Lancs	Professional	23"	White
3160	Norman Sullivan Ltd., Sheffield	Professional	24"	Eau de Nil
4160	Dave Midgley, Thurcroft	Professional	24"	
5160	F.R. Russell, Walsall	Professional	22"	Tangerine
6160	M.A. James Cycles, Alford, Lincs	Professional Track	22"	White
7160	A. Geddis Cycles, Belfast	Conquest	24"	Blue
8160	M. Dalton, Sheffield	Professional	23"	Yellow
9160	J.A. Webster Cycles, Chesterfield	Conquest	23"	White
10160	J.A. Webster Cycles, Chesterfield	Conquest	22"	Blue
11160	Otley Cycle Depot, Otley	Conquest R/P	22 ½"	Green
12160	Cliff Pratt Cycles, Hull	Conquest R/P	23"	Eau de Nil
13160	Cliff Pratt Cycles, Hull	Conquest	20 ½"	Blue
14160	A. Geddis Cycles, Belfast	Conquest	20"	Red
15160	J.R. Mansley, Liverpool	Professional	24"	Silver
16160	J. Mullins, Maltby	Conquest	21 ½"	White
17160	Matt Newton Ltd., Middlesbrough	Professional	24 ½"	Purple
18160	A.M. Bird, Bolton on Dearn	Professional	22"	Orange
19160	A. Lynne Cycles, Sheffield	Professional	23 ¾"	Green
20160	Dave Lee, Sheffield	Professional	22"	Green
21160	Roger Macrae Cycles, Edinburgh	Conquest R/P	23"	Gold
22160	Roger Macrae Cycles, Edinburgh	Professional	23"	Purple
23160	Norman Sullivan Ltd., Sheffield	Professional	24"	Orange
24160	M.L. Jones, Cannock, Staffs	Conquest	21"	White
25160	I. Bagley, Maltby	Conquest	25"	Pink
26160	M. Ibbotson, Sheffield	Conquest R/P	23"	Black
27260	Horton & Hollinder, Wetherby	Conquest R/P	23 ½"	Green
28260	W.T. Hammond & Co, Worcester	Professional	24"	Blue
29260	J. Cooper, Chapeltown	Conquest	25"	Blue
30260	Denton Cycles, Newcastle on Tyne	Professional R/P	24 ½"	Blue
31260	Norman Sullivan Ltd., Sheffield	Conquest	23"	Blue
32260	Norman Sullivan Ltd., Sheffield	Conquest	23"	Ruby
33260	Norman Sullivan Ltd.; Sheffield	Conquest	23"	Purple
34260	Robt. Fletcher Cycles, Sheffield	Professional	22 ½"	Orange
35260	N.E. Sylvester, Lincoln	Professional	20"	Chrome

NUMBER	ORDER	MODEL	SIZE	COLOUR
36360	Leedham & Son, Leicester	Conquest	21"	Yellow
37360	B. Lines, Renishaw	Conquest	22 ½"	Grey
38360	N. Terrington, Dronfield	Professional	26"	Blue
39360	P.G. Wanby, Leeds	Conquest	24"	Blue
40360	M.A. James Cycles, Alford, Lincs	Professional	22"	Cerise
41360	A.C. Mundy Cycles, Peterborough	Professional	25"	Blue
42360	Bev Wood, Droylesden, Lancs	Professional	22 ½"	White
43360	A.E. Wells Cycles, Sheffield	Professional	23"	
44360	stock	Conquest	23"	
45360	stock	Conquest	23"	
46360	stock	Conquest	23"	
47360	stock	Conquest	23"	
48360	stock	Conquest	23"	
49360	stock	Conquest	22"	
50360	stock	Conquest	22"	
51360	stock	Conquest	22"	
52360	stock	Conquest	22"	
53360	stock	Conquest	22"	
54460	M.R. Bushby, Hessle, Yorks	Professional	22 ½"	Green
55460	Ron Cookham, Sheffield	Professional	22 ½"	Silver/blue
56460	C.D. Robson Cycles, Manchester	Conquest	22 ½"	Orange
57460	John Badham, Rotherham	Conquest	21"	Black
58560	Solo Cycles, Peterborough	Professional	22"	Pink
59560	Cowan's Cycles, Manchester	Professional	25"	White
60760	Highgate Cycles, Cleethorpes	Professional	24"	Orange
61760	M. Taylor, Sheffield	Professional	24"	Orange
62760	W. Evans, Sheffield	Conquest	26"	Green
63760	Cliff Pratt Ltd., Hull	Conquest R/P	24"	White
64860	Highgate Cycles, Cleethorpes	Professional	23"	Orange
65860	W. Mason, Sheffield	Professional	24"	Silver/red
66860	D.L. Walley, Sheffield	Conquest	23"	Ruby
67960	Cliff Pratt Cycles, Hull	Conquest	22"	Green
68960	Blagden, Stocksbridge	Conquest	24"	Copper flam.
69960	Denton Cycles, Newcastle on Tyne	Professional	22"	Red
70960	Cliff Pratt Ltd., Hull	Conquest	23"	Lilac
71960	A. Geddis Cycles, Belfast	Professional	21"	Ruby
72960	D. Dalton, Deepcar	Conquest	25"	Blue
73960	David Lee (prize), Wilmslow	Professional	22"	Black
741060	J.A. Webster Cycles, Chesterfield	Conquest	24"	Duck egg blue
751060	A. Pidcock, Sheffield	Conquest	22"	White
761060	Highgate Cycles, Cleethorpes	Professional	22"	Black
771060	C.D. Robson Cycles, Manchester	Professional	22"	Pale green
781060	Norman Sullivan Ltd., Sheffield	Professional	24"	Lilac
791160	W.E. Dobson, Sheffield	Professional	23"	Orange
801160	C. Jones, Sheffield	Professional	24"	Blue

NUMBER	ORDER	MODEL	SIZE	COLOUR
811160	Denton Cycles, Newcastle on Tyne	Professional	22 ½"	Bianchi blue
821160	M.A. James Cycles, Alford, Lincs	Conquest	22"	Grey
831160	B. Crabtree, Conisborough	Conquest	23 ½"	Ruby
841160	J.A. Webster Cycles, Chesterfield	Professional	23 ½"	Blue
851160	stock	Professional	23"	Blue
861160	B. Liversidge, Sheffield	Professional	24"	Orange
871260	A. Geddis Cycles, Belfast	Professional	20"	Green
881260	Denton Cycles, Newcastle on Tyne	Professional	22 ½"	Green
891260	Doug Drake, Sheffield	Professional	23"	Green
901260	Norman Sullivan Ltd., Sheffield	Professional	24"	White

1961 FRAMES

NUMBER	ORDER	MODEL	SIZE	COLOUR
1161	Mr. D. Spencer, Sheffield	Conquest	23 ½"	Black
2161	Bagley, Maltby	Conquest R/P	25"	Pink
3161	stock	Professional	23"	Orange
4161	stock	Professional	23"	Blue
5161	stock	Professional	24"	Green
6161	stock	Conquest	23"	White/orange
7161	J.A. Webster Cycles, Chesterfield	Conquest	24"	Tangerine
8261	J.R. Mansley, Liverpool	Professional	24"	Silver/blue
9261	D. Rolfe, Barnsley	Conquest	22"	White
10261	W.S. Maples (Cycles), Lincoln	Conquest	23"	Blue
11261	A.W. Fuller, Rotherham	Professional	22"	Black
12361	Denton Cycles, Newcastle on Tyne	Professional	22"	Blue
13361	A. Geddis Cycles, Belfast	Conquest	22"	Blue
14361	A. Geddis Cycles, Belfast	Conquest	22"	Green
15361	A. Geddis Cycles, Belfast	Conquest	23"	Orange
16361	A. Geddis Cycles, Belfast	Conquest	23"	Lilac
17361	A. Geddis Cycles, Belfast	Conquest	24"	Blue
18361	A. Geddis Cycles, Belfast	Conquest	21"	White
19361	stock	Professional	23 ½"	White
20361	Laundbury & Sons, Boston, Linc	Conquest R/P	22"	Green
21361	Highgate Cycles, Cleethorpes	Professional	23 ½"	White
22461	J.A. Webster Cycles, Chesterfield	Conquest	22"	Blue
23461	stock	Conquest	23"	Orange
24461	stock	Conquest	23"	Orange
25461	stock	Conquest	24"	Red
26461	J.A. Webster Cycles, Chesterfield	Conquest	22"	Blue
27561	Norman Sullivan Ltd., Sheffield Sheffield	Conquest	24"	Orange
28561	Norman Sullivan Ltd., Sheffield	Professional	24"	White
29561	W.S. Maples Cycles, Lincoln	Conquest R/P	23"	Orange

NUMBER	ORDER	MODEL	SIZE	COLOUR
30561	P.R. Rudd, Sheffield	Conquest	25"	White
31561	Denton Cycles, Newcastle on Tyne	Professional	22 ½"	Mushroom
32561	Jack Kirk Ltd., Hull	Conquest	21"	Blue
33661	J. Brownhill, Sheffield	Professional	23"	Blue
34661	Solo Cycles, Peterborough	Professional	22"	Yellow
35761	J. Bacon, Sheffield	Professional	23 ½"	Orange
36761	J.C. Walters, Sheffield	Professional	24"	White
37761	A. Geddis Cycles, Belfast	Conquest	22"	White
38761	A. Geddis Cycles, Belfast	Conquest	23"	Orange
39761	A. Geddis Cycles, Belfast	Conquest	23"	Green
40861	Len Raine Cycles, Scarborough	Professional	22"	Red
41861	Denton Cycles, Newcastle on Tyne	Professional	21"	Red
42861	Arthur Wilson, Sheffield	Professional R/P	20 ½"	Blue
43861	K. Hargreaves, Sheffield	Professional	23"	Green
44861	Cliff Pratt Ltd., Hull	Professional	23"	Green
45861	P. Gasiorski, Rotherham	Professional	22"	White
46961	Jack Kirk Ltd., Hull	Professional R/P	23"	White
47961	S. Fletcher, Stockport	Professional	21 ½"	White
48961	Highgate Cycles, Cleethorpes	Professional	23 ½"	Lime green
491061	Cliff Pratt Ltd., Hull	Conquest	24"	Purple flam.
501061	Cliff Pratt Ltd., Hull	Conquest	24"	Blue
511061	K.A. Lyne Cycles, Sheffield	Conquest	23 ½"	
521261	J.A. Webster Cycles, Chesterfield	Professional	21 ½"	Maroon
531261	Denton Cycles, Newcastle on Tyne	Professional	22"	Blue

1962 FRAMES

NUMBER	ORDER	MODEL	SIZE	COLOUR
1162	A.E. Butterworth Cycles, Sheffield	Conquest	24"	Blue
2262	L.H. Dodd, Sheffield	Professional	21 ¼"	Bronze
3262	Harvey, Sheffield	Conquest	23"	Blue
4362	G. Lawrence, Sheffield	Professional	24"	Red
5462	J.A. Webster Cycles, Chesterfield	Conquest	24"	Dark blue
6462	J.A. Webster Cycles, Chesterfield	Conquest	22"	Light blue
7462	S. Ward, Sheffield	Professional	24 ½"	Red
8462	Denton Cycles, Newcastle on Tyne	Professional	22 ½"	Blue
9562	M. Brown, Sheffield	Conquest	23"	Orange
10562	B. Pashley, Sheffield	Professional	22"	Orange
11562	M. Davidson, Sheffield	Conquest	23"	Green
12662	J.A. Webster Cycles, Chesterfield	Conquest	24"	Blue
13862	B.A. Hodson Cycles, Leeds	Professional	22"	Blue
14962	D.W. Dungworth, Sheffield	Professional	22"	Kingfisher
15962	M.A. James Cycles, Alford, Lincs	Professional	23 ½"	Blue

NUMBER	ORDER	MODEL	SIZE	COLOUR
16962	Denton Cycles, Newcastle on Tyne	Professional	22 ½"	Copper
17962	R. Clarke, Sheffield	Conquest	23 ½"	Citrus yellow
18962	Stephen Housley, Sheffield	Conquest	22 ½"	White

1963-1964 FRAMES not made in the Langsett workshop.

NUMBER	ORDER	MODEL	SIZE	COLOUR
4608	C. Martys, Sheffield	Professional	23 ½"	Silver grey
4610		Professional	23 ½"	Blue poly.
4609		Conquest	23"	Blue flam.
64081		Conquest	23"	Grey